Contents

Race, Religion, and Economic Change in the Republican South

UNIVERSITY PRESS OF FLORIDA

Florida A&M University, Tallahassee
Florida Atlantic University, Boca Raton
Florida Gulf Coast University, Ft. Myers
Florida International University, Miami
Florida State University, Tallahassee
New College of Florida, Sarasota
University of Central Florida, Orlando
University of Florida, Gainesville
University of North Florida, Jacksonville
University of South Florida, Tampa
University of West Florida, Pensacola

Race, Religion, and Economic Change in the Republican South

A Study of a Southern City

Matthew T. Corrigan

University Press of Florida
Gainesville/Tallahassee/Tampa/Boca Raton
Pensacola/Orlando/Miami/Jacksonville/Ft. Myers/Sarasota

13 12 11 10 09 08   6 5 4 3 2 1

Library of Congress Cataloging-in-Publication Data
Corrigan, Matthew T.
Race, religion, and economic change in the Republican South :
a case study of a southern city / Matthew T. Corrigan.
p. cm.
Includes bibliographical references and index.
ISBN 978-0-8130-3160-6 (cloth)
ISBN 978-0-8130-3314-3 (pbk.)
1. Jacksonville (Fla.)—Race relations. 2. Jacksonville (Fla.)—
Politics and government. 3. Republican Party (U.S. : 1854-)
4. Political leadership—Florida—Jacksonville. 5. Religion and politics—Florida—
Jacksonville. 6. Jacksonville (Fla.)—Economic conditions. 7. Southern States—
Race relations—Case studies. 8. Southern States—Politics and government—Case
studies. 9. Political leadership—Southern States—Case studies. 10. Southern
States—Economic conditions—Case studies. I. Title.
F319.J1C67   2007
305.8009759'12—dc22   2007016623

The University Press of Florida is the scholarly publishing agency for the State
University System of Florida, comprising Florida A&M University, Florida Atlantic
University, Florida Gulf Coast University, Florida International University, Florida
State University, New College of Florida, University of Central Florida, University
of Florida, University of North Florida, University of South Florida, and University
of West Florida.

University Press of Florida
15 Northwest 15th Street
Gainesville, FL 32611-2079
http://www.upf.com

This book is dedicated to my wife, Mary, and my son, John.

Thank you for your love and support. You are my favorite Southerners.

Tables

Maps

Illustrations

Acknowledgments

The first place any acknowledgment should begin is with my parents, John and Patricia Corrigan. It is with their love and support that my education was made possible.

Meredith Morris Babb and Eli Bortz at the University Press of Florida have supported this book from its inception. Their encouragement has made this project more rewarding.

I also owe a tremendous debt to my graduate school professors at the University of Florida. They encouraged me to ask important and comprehensive questions. I would like to particularly thank Jim Button and Richard Scher. Professor Button unfortunately died in 2005. He wrote a terrific book, *Blacks and Social Change*. He encouraged me to research the important issues of race and economic change. Professor Scher continually has supported me through my graduate years and professional career. His works on Southern politics have inspired me.

At the University of North Florida, I want to thank Mark Workman and David Jaffee for their financial support for a Dean's Faculty Fellowship and a semester sabbatical. My colleagues in the Department of Political Science and Public Administration have been good friends and encouraging supporters. In particular, Henry Thomas and Ted Stumm offered encouragement for this project during their terms as chairs. My deceased friend Terry Bowen also was a strong colleague and supporter. Terry is dearly missed.

Without the Public Opinion Laboratory at UNF, this project would not have been possible. Thank you to Adam Herbert, now the current president of Indiana University, for establishing the lab during his leadership of the Florida Center. I have been fortunate to have an excellent staff at the lab. Jacci Dorey has been a tremendous help in formatting the manuscript. Mark Swanhart assisted me consistently with data analysis and presentation. I thank them for their quality of work and dedication. Janie Smalley helped establish the lab and supervised part of this project. Over fifty UNF undergraduates assisted in data collection for this project. I am glad they earned a little money while learning about social science research.

Finally, David Wilson at the Center for Instruction and Research Technology at UNF was a tremendous asset in formatting the figures and maps in the book. The Center for Community Initiatives at UNF provided the GIS analysis that created the maps in the book.

I offer great appreciation to Professor Glen Broward and Professor Stephen Baker for their reviews and comments. They made this work better, but I am responsible for any errors.

1

Introduction

The South as a Political Region

"I'm going to carry the South because the people understand that . . . we share values . . . they know me well. I believe I did well in the South last time and will do well in the South this time because the senator from Massachusetts does not share their values" (United Press International 2004). This comment by Republican president George W. Bush during the 2004 presidential election sums up his argument against his Democratic opponent in the region of the country that was once known as the "Democratic Solid South." Bush had reason to be confident. He had won every state of the old Confederacy in the year 2000 when the disputed Florida election results were settled. In 2004 he was facing a Massachusetts senator who had said earlier in the primary race that Democrats did not need to win the South to win the presidency. While John Kerry's statement was factually true, this non-Southern strategy would force Democrats to try to win 70% of the remaining electoral votes in the nation (Black and Black 1992). This standard was not met when John Kerry conceded the state of Ohio and the race on November 3, 2004.

The fact that a Democratic presidential candidate would essentially write off the South highlights the tremendous changes in Southern politics in the more than fifty years since V. O. Key (1949) wrote his seminal work on Southern politics that described a region dominated by a Democratic Party that was intent on preserving racial segregation and economic exploitation. Despite his bleak description, Key believed that an analysis of Southern politics was crucial because he saw promise in the region:

> The South is our last frontier. In the development of its resources, both human and natural, must be found the next great epoch of our national growth (Key 1949, 4).

In short, Key viewed the development of the South as being in concert with the development of democracy in the United States. Given these important implications, it is necessary to continually examine the region's political trends and results. In the mid-twentieth century, Key found a region that "as a whole had developed no system or practice of political organization and leadership adequate to cope with its problems" (Key 1949, 4). This lack of political leadership in the South left a system that centered on maintaining power among a few white elites. Racial separation was the glue that held Southern political power together. The noncompetitive, segregated system of the 1940s left the South unable or unwilling to confront the problems of the social and economic legacies of the Civil War.

More than 50 years later, the South that Key described has undergone fundamental changes. Republicans now dominate most of the region. Republicans have swept the 11-state South in the last two presidential elections. These states include Alabama, Arkansas, Georgia, Florida, Louisiana, Mississippi, North Carolina, South Carolina, Tennessee, Texas, and Virginia. Even after the Democratic victories in the 2006 Congressional elections, Republicans hold 6 out of 11 gubernatorial offices, 17 out of 22 U.S. Senate seats, and nearly 65% of U.S. House seats. Interestingly, the Democratic electoral nationwide success in 2006 has even further highlighted the strength of Republicans in the South. The Southern region was the Republican firewall against the Democratic wave of the 2006 elections, with Republicans winning five out of seven governors' offices and losing only one Virginia Senate seat and three U.S. House seats in the region (two of these seats were in South Florida). In fact, Democrats have struggled so much in the region that some observers have suggested that Democrats give up on the South and focus their energies elsewhere (Schaller 2006).

Earl Black and Merle Black (2000) described a region that has been transformed politically and economically. The loss of many white conservatives and moderates among Democrats in the South has made the Republican Party a dominant political power. Since 1964, Democratic Party identification in the South has dropped 30 percentage points while Republican Party identification has gained nearly as much (Black and Black 1987).

These changes in Southern politics have been well-documented by a list of gifted scholars. The important works of V. O. Key and Earl and Merle Black are mentioned above. Alexander Heard (1952) wrote one of the earliest books on the possibility of a two-party South. Bass and DeVries (1975) interviewed more than 360 elected officials from the South and found that fundamental political change was coming. Charles Bullock and Mark Rozell (2003) have documented how the South has become the most important region for the Republican Party. Green et al. (2003) have written about how white Protestants have flocked to the Republican Party in droves.

However, fewer scholars have studied the consequences of these radical changes in Southern politics. Lublin (1997) examines some of the unintended effects of racial redistricting. Scher (1997) makes the important contribution of examining some of the possible economic and social impacts of the new Southern political order. This present study seeks to contribute to the discussion about two central questions: Does it matter that Republicans are now in control? And, to update a question about Democrats posed by Key 50 years ago, Is the new political South led by the Republican Party rising to the challenge of providing a political system to meet the region's problems and opportunities?

These questions are important because while many political observers have dissected the electoral rise of Republicans in the South, they have not examined the potential consequences of that rise. Key's seminal work was an outstanding explanatory examination of the state of Southern politics. However, it also was an analysis with a purpose. His finding that the political system in the South was broken mattered greatly because of the backward condition of the region at the time. Similarly, it is important for today's political analysts to examine the possible impacts of the new Southern political system, which has a strong Republican advantage.

This study finds that the ways that Republicans in the region have gained political power may have important impacts on governing. The political coalition that Republicans have relied on to win elections in the South presents important challenges in leading a section of the nation with a difficult social and political history. The coalition that Republicans have put together has left Democrats more isolated politically in the South than they have been at any time in American political history.

To adequately address these issues, three interacting streams of Southern politics must be examined: 1) racial politics; 2) economic changes in the region; and 3) the interaction of religion and politics. John Kingdon (1984) discussed how policy streams come together to make public policy. In the South, the three streams of race, economy, and religion determine who will be elected and how he or she will govern. A complete analysis of Southern politics must include all three factors.

Why attempt to incorporate all three factors in one study? Many outstanding political scientists have described partisan change in the South and provided reasons for this change. Edward Carmines and James Stimson

(1989) focused on race as the impetus for Republican growth in the South. Byron Shafer and Richard Johnson (2006) wrote about economic change as being crucial to the rise of the Republicans. John Green and James Guth (1991) explained the central roles of religion and morality in Southern politics.

This examination of Southern politics does not focus on one variable as the preeminent characteristic of Southern politics. Examination of survey data yields differing results about the impetus for partisan change. Yet few could argue with the fundamental idea that race, religion, and economic change are all critical to understanding Southern politics. Racial differences play powerful roles in Southern politics and accelerated the movement toward the Republican Party in the 1960s; however, the politics of religion and economic change also helped cement this shift. To understand the consequences of these dramatic changes, all three concepts must be examined. To study one without considering the other two would be like attempting to solve a jigsaw puzzle without having all the pieces.

This study will look at all three factors from two perspectives: 1) an examination of attitudes of the entire South; and 2) an intensive case study of Jacksonville, Florida, as an example of a Southern city whose politics have been transformed by race, religion, and economics.

The data examined are from more than 2,000 interviews conducted by phone using a stratified sample with random digit dialing technology. A total of 803 interviews were conducted with voters in the 11-state South. More than 1,200 interviews were conducted with voters in Jacksonville, Florida, including an oversample of African Americans for comparison purposes. Voters are defined as citizens who vote in presidential elections. A detailed methodology is available in the appendices. First, general patterns in Southern politics will be highlighted by examining regionwide data; then these patterns will be further explored in depth in the case study.

While exploring these issues is important to scholars of Southern politics, it may be more important to the nation. In many ways, the future development of the South will determine the economic and political course of the United States (Applebome 1996).

Race

Has the change in the political structure of the South addressed the issue of racial separation in the region's politics? In the post-civil rights era (after 1965), have African Americans been fully integrated into the South's politi-

Table 1.1. Race and Party Identification

	White[a]	Black[b]
Democrat	30.1%	79.8%
Republican	44.4%	3.7%
Independent	20.9%	9.2%
Other	4.7%	7.3%

Source: Survey of Southern Voters, June 2004. Public Opinion Research Laboratory, University of North Florida.
Note: Whites vs. Blacks signification at $P \leq .05$ chi^2 statistic.
[a] $N = 599$
[b] $N = 109$

cal system? As Key stipulated in his seminal work, any analysis of Southern politics must begin with the issue of race relations. Today Key's analysis is still correct, but in ways he could not have imagined. Instead of being disenfranchised and excluded from politics, African Americans are active and vibrant participants in Southern politics. In fact, African Americans are the base of the Democratic Party in the South (Greenblatt 2003). Moreover, over 5,000 black elected officials now serve in the region where blacks were once blocked from going to the polls (many of these officials come from places with a high proportion of African Americans in the population). The greatest numbers of black elected officials are in the former strongholds of segregation, Mississippi and Alabama (Bositis 2001). In the 1970s and 1980s, African Americans and white Democrats formed voting coalitions that kept Democrats in power in most offices in the South below the presidential level. Even today, these coalitions allow Democrats to remain competitive in state legislative and gubernatorial races in many Southern states.

With this active participation, why is race still so central to Southern politics? The migration of white Southerners to the Republican Party during the last forty years has created a new racial divide in Southern politics. The difference between white and black Southerners is no longer enforced by Jim Crow laws that legally exclude blacks from participating in politics. Instead, this racial separation is one of political choice, with more whites aligning with Republicans in the South and African Americans staying with the Democratic Party in overwhelming numbers.

Table 1.1 highlights this separation. In a survey of Southern voters, when asked about their registration, 86% of African Americans were registered as Democrats and 79% identified themselves as Democrats. A strong plurality of whites are now registered as Republicans, and 44% identify themselves with the GOP.

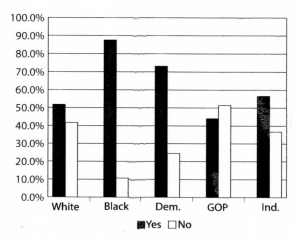

Figure 1.1. Bar chart of racial and partisan breakdown of responses to the question, "Do you believe that African Americans experience racial discrimination in their daily lives?" Survey of Southern Voters, 2004, Public Opinion Research Laboratory at the University of North Florida, $N = 803$.

Actual voting results reveal a stronger pattern. This pattern is highlighted by exit polls of voters in the 2000 and 2004 presidential elections. According to the 2000 election exit polls, an astounding 67% of whites supported the Bush/Cheney ticket, and 90% of African Americans supported the Gore/Lieberman ticket.[i] The numbers in 2004 showed the exact same pattern, with Bush receiving more than 70% of the white vote and Kerry receiving almost 90% of the African American vote.

With these patterns of Republican gains among whites in the South, white independent votes become more important to Democrats to remain competitive. However, when white independents were asked in the University of North Florida survey, "As an independent, do you lean to the Democratic Party or the Republican Party?" white Southern independents cite the Republican Party over the Democratic Party by a 2–1 margin.

These divisions show the importance of a race dynamic in Southern politics. This dynamic is an extension of attitudes about race in the South. Both whites and blacks see discrimination as a current problem for African Americans, as shown in figure 1.1.

Yet their views on government action to address discrimination differ vastly. As table 1.2 illustrates, only 27% of whites believe that affirmative

Table 1.2. Which of the Following Statements Comes Closest to Your Views about Affirmative Action?

	Race[a]		Political Party Identification[b]		
	White	Black	Dem.	GOP	Ind.
Affirmative action is needed	26.6%	79.3%	56.4%	16.5%	33.8%
Affirmative action is not needed	61.5%	9.9%	31.4%	73.5%	55.2%
Do not know	11.9%	10.8%	12.1%	10.0%	11.0%

Source: Survey of Southern Voters, June 2004. Public Opinion Research Laboratory, University of North Florida.
Note: Race and political party signification at $P \leq .05$ chi^2 statistic.
[a] $N = 732$
[b] $N = 777$

action programs are needed to address discrimination, while 79% of African Americans say that they are needed. Moreover, only 17% of Republican identifiers think affirmative action is needed, and a majority does not believe African Americans experience discrimination. Democrats show exactly the opposite trends. Thus, the racial polarization of political parties in the South is accompanied by a sharp division of opinion on government assistance to African Americans and other minorities.

If the Republicans maintain their majority position in the South, African Americans may see less in terms of affirmative action programs such as contracting, educational assistance, and set-asides. African Americans see a clear problem that discrimination still exists, but a majority of Republican voters does not believe that discrimination is a current dilemma. Thus, they are much less likely to support affirmative action programs. Accordingly office-holders who are elected by Republican majorities have little incentive to respond to the African American community. For example, former governor Jeb Bush instituted a policy to replace affirmative action programs in the state of Florida. His "One Florida" initiative was roundly criticized by black leaders and led to a large protest march on the capitol in Tallahassee (Hallifax 2003).

In short, African Americans do not support Republican candidates, and Republican voters do not support affirmative action. This reality is increasingly making African Americans a majority racial group in the minority political party in many parts of the South. This dynamic has important consequences for the future of politics in the region.

Religion and Morality

In the past 25 years, white Protestant churches have joined African American churches as centers of political activity in the South. This grassroots activity at the church level has been combined with a mass-market approach that highlights character and morality as important aspects of political advertising through the outlets of television, radio, direct mail, and the Internet. Political consultants have made high-profile morality issues a central part of campaigns in the South. Issues such as gay marriage, various limitations on abortions, and religious symbols in public spaces have been used to separate Democrats and Republicans. White Protestant and Catholic churches have become central to the Republican Party's get-out-the-vote efforts. Both African American and white ministers and priests have become extremely vocal and public about their political preferences. Finally, the Bush campaign made the courting of white Christian conservatives a cornerstone of the 2000 and 2004 Republican presidential campaigns (Abcarian 2005).

All of these factors combined to strengthen the connection between religion/morality and politics among Southern voters. This connection is very evident in table 1.3. In keeping with the traditions of the civil rights movement and its base in Southern churches, black voters show a clear pattern between religion and political beliefs. Clear majorities of Democrats and Republicans believe that religious values have an important connection with their political philosophy. However, these voters may disagree on which religious values should be applied to politics. For example, some voters consider abortion a more pressing issue than poverty and vice versa. Yet,

Table 1.3. How Important Are Your Religious Values in Determining Your Political Beliefs?

	Political Party Race[a]		Identification[b]		
	White	Black	Dem.	GOP	Ind.
Very important	44.0%	64.8%	3.6%	56.5%	2.1%
Somewhat important	29.5%	25.0%	30.3%	25.0%	35.8%
Somewhat unimportant	11.1%	4.6%	12.1%	7.6%	8.8%
Very unimportant	15.4%	5.6%	14.0%	10.9%	23.4%

Source: Survey of Southern Voters, June 2004. Public Opinion Research Laboratory, University of North Florida.
Note: Race and party identification significant at $P \leq .05$ chi^2 statistic.
[a] $N = 704$
[b] $N = 677$

Table 1.4. How Important Is It to You that the President of the United States Be a Religious Person?

	Political Party Race[a]		Identification[b]		
	White	Black	Dem.	GOP	Ind.
Very important	51.9%	56.0%	41.9%	66.2%	39.0%
Somewhat important	25.2%	27.5%	28.5%	22.1%	30.8%
Somewhat unimportant	9.4%	5.5%	11.6%	6.4%	10.3%
Very unimportant	13.5%	11.0%	18.1%	5.3%	19.9%

Source: Survey of Southern Voters, June 2004. Public Opinion Research Laboratory, University of North Florida.
Note: Party identification significant at P ≤ .05 chi^2 statistic.
[a] $N = 729$
[b] $N = 704$

Table 1.5. How Concerned Are You that the Moral Values of the United States Are Declining?

	Political Party Race[a]		Identification[b]		
	White	Black	Dem.	GOP	Ind.
Very concerned	69.5%	75.9%	62.5%	78.1%	69.4%
Somewhat concerned	21.0%	20.4%	25.6%	16.3%	20.1%
Somewhat unconcerned	5.0%	3.7%	7.6%	3.5%	4.9%
Very unconcerned	4.5%	0.0%	4.3%	2.1%	5.6%

Source: Survey of Southern Voters, June 2004. Public Opinion Research Laboratory, University of North Florida.
Note: Party identification significant at P ≤ .05 chi^2 statistic.
[a] $N = 728$
[b] $N = 704$

regardless of their positions, a majority of white and black Southerners and Democrats and Republicans agree that a connection is there.

Likewise, many Southern voters want this connection between religion and politics to be evident among political candidates. Table 1.4 highlights the importance of religion in influencing voters' judgment about the president of the United States. Again, both blacks and whites, Democrats and Republicans believe that it is important for the president to be a religious person. Slightly more than 66% of Republicans believe that this presidential characteristic is very important.

The data in this table may help explain the different ways that Senator Kerry and President Bush responded to questions about religion during the 2004 campaign. Bush often talked about his Christian faith and "how [it]

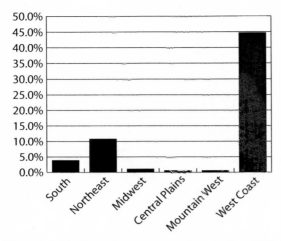

Figure 1.2. Bar chart of responses to the question, "Which area of the nation has the weakest moral values?" Survey of Southern Voters, 2004, Public Opinion Research Laboratory at the University of North Florida, $N = 803$.

guides his decision-making" (Straub 2004, 4). Kerry, however, struggled with this aspect of his campaign. He was not as comfortable talking about his Catholic religion and he also found himself in the unusual position of being in conflict with Catholic bishops on the issue of abortion throughout the 2004 campaign. Many Southerners want an outward sign of the president's commitment to his religion, and Bush delivered.

Moreover, issues of morality and religion have great saliency with Southern voters. When voters were asked if they were concerned about the decline of morality in the United States, clear majorities of whites and African Americans, Democrats and Republicans said yes. 78% of Republicans said they were very concerned. With topics such as gay marriage dominating public dialogue in 2004, Southern voters made strong connections between moral/religious convictions and political beliefs.

However, Southern voters did not see fellow Southerners as the most moral citizens in the country. When asked if Southerners had stronger moral values than the rest of the country, most Southerners did not agree. Nevertheless, when asked which region of the country has the *weakest* moral values, figure 1.2 shows that the West Coast has a clear plurality. Southern Republicans show a greater level of distrust with the West Coast than do Democrats. This trend helps explain how Kerry and John Edwards, the vice presidential candidate, were branded during the 2004 campaign with having "Hollywood values" (Johnson 2004). Many Southerners distrust Hollywood, and Republicans continually deliver that message to Southern voters.

While commentators, academics, and pollsters argue about the separation of church and state, these data suggest that most Southerners have made up their minds that religion and politics are intertwined. How Southern voters interpret the words *morality* and *values* is, of course, crucial to this analysis. As Green et al. (2003) have shown, variation exists between Southern white Protestants, Southern black Protestants, and other religious groups regarding religion and its connection to political behavior. What varies little is the strong connection that most Southerners draw between religion and politics. These data show that: 1) morality and religion are important to Southern voters, and they are concerned about the morality of the nation; 2) moral and religious views of voters do impact their political beliefs; and 3) Southern voters expect morality and religion to be important parts of a political candidate's background and makeup. Candidates cannot offer *only* their religious beliefs as a basis for voter appeals, but the connection between religion and political beliefs is vital. All of these factors have given Republicans a strong advantage in the region when political discussion turns to religion and morality.

Economic Change

One of V. O. Key's central ideas was that Southern political leaders had failed their fellow citizens due to the widespread poverty that afflicted the region during the first half of the twentieth century. The tenant-sharecropping model that dominated the region's agricultural economy created a system of economic elites with a large lower class (Scher 1997). This system with a few wealthy landowners and a mass of agricultural workers led to poverty for whites and blacks alike. The South was the nation's economic bad case. Industrialization and urbanization helped to transform the region and gradually diversify the region's economy. Yet, hostility to unions among Southern governments did not allow manufacturing workers to earn nearly the wages that Northern blue-collar workers could get (Scher 1997).

The term *New South* was used to describe the Southern economy and society in the post-civil rights period (post 1964). The New South's economy became even more diversified due to the combination of new people moving to the South, increased technology, and advances in transportation. This diversified economy included real estate and homebuilding, tourism,

Table 1.6. Current Southerners and Length of Time in the South

Less than 1 year	1.9%
1 to 5 years	3.6%
6 to 10 years	4.8%
11 to 20 years	9.2%
More than 20 years	31.7%
Native Southerner	48.9%

Source: Survey of Southern Voters, 2004. Public Opinion Research Laboratory, University of North Florida.
Note: N = 801

military expenditures, oil and natural resources, technology, agribusiness, international trade, and banking (Sale 1975; Black and Black 1987).

It is difficult to overstate the depth of economic change in the region during the last 40 years. During this period, the South has led the United States in job and population growth compared to other regions of the country. Only about 1% of the South's working population is now employed on a farm. The per capita income of the region is now almost the same as that

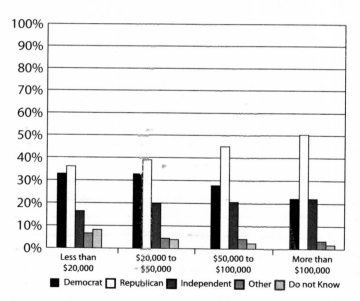

Figure 1.3. Bar chart of party identification by income group (whites only). Survey of Southern Voters, 2004, Public Opinion Research Laboratory at the University of North Florida, *N* = 642.

of the rest of the nation (Dodson et al 2004). Metropolitan areas with cities and their surrounding suburbs now dominate the South's economy. Because most Southern states have right-to-work laws, fewer regulations, and lower tax burdens than do other parts of the country, more foreign and domestic businesses have relocated to the South.

Once the domain of a small group of elite landowners and millions of poor Southerners, the region now has a thriving middle class and upper-middle class. Many of the South's new residents moved there for economic opportunity (Black and Black 1987). Table 1.6 shows that native Southern-ers no longer constitute a clear majority of the population.[2] Citizens from other parts of the United States, particularly the Midwest and Northeast, have brought with them their own political ideas and search for economic opportunity. These population shifts present a difficult scenario for Demo-crats. If new migrants from other parts of the country continually give an edge to Republicans, Democrats will find it difficult to regain their footing in the South.

Black and Black state that the white middle class has transformed the politics of the region. The data in Figure 1.3 demonstrate that among whites, all income groups indicate a Republican plurality in party identification. Even among the lower class, the Republicans have an advantage, and among the upper middle class ($50,000 and above), they have a wide advantage. This trend is problematic for the Democratic Party, which for most of the twentieth century used the New Deal as the foundation of its power. The Democratic coalition was made up of African Americans, immigrants, union members, and Southerners who differed on many social and racial issues in the 1930s but came together under the New Deal economic um-brella.

Some data suggest that Democrats should be able to make an economic argument. Even in the most conservative part of the country, Democrats remain competitive on economic issues. When asked, Which party do you trust on economic issues?, Democrats win all income groups except those earning $100,000 or more per year (table 1.7).

Moreover, even though the South has become more prosperous in the last several decades, it still remains the poorest region in the nation. In *Dis-mantling Persistent Poverty*, a report examining poverty in 7 of the 11 South-ern states, a team of social scientists studied 217 contiguous rural Southern counties from Mississippi to Florida to North Carolina (Ledbetter 2004). These counties are similar to the "Black Belt" described in numerous analy-

Table 1.7. Which Political Party Do You Trust More on Economic Issues?

	Less than $20K[a]	$20K to $50K[b]	$50K to $100K[c]	More than $100K[d]
Republican	27.8%	36.8%	41.2%	54.5%
Democratic	58.8%	48.7%	42.3%	31.1%
Neither	3.1%	7.0%	9.2%	8.3%
Both equally	2.1%	3.5%	2.7%	3.0%
Do not know	8.2%	3.9%	4.6%	3.0%

Source: Survey of Southern Voters, June 2004. Public Opinion Research Laboratory, University of North Florida.
Note: P ≤ .05 chi^2 statistic.
[a] $N = 97$
[b] $N = 228$
[c] $N = 260$
[d] $N = 132$

ses of Southern politics. While the population of African Americans is high in comparison with other parts of the nation, whites are the clear majority (62%) in these distressed counties, illustrating that poverty impacts both black and white Southerners. These counties have a poverty rate almost double that of the nation. The technological and communication advances that have aided the economy of the South have not had a dramatic impact in these counties.

With the growth of urbanized areas, the numbers of urban poor have increased throughout the region as well. As a result, income inequality is an important social phenomenon in the region. In the post-civil rights period, Southern states have populations with widening income gaps (Morill 2000). An examination of recent poverty rates shows that 8 out of 11 Southern states have poverty rates higher than the national average (see table 1.8).

Given these economic realities, Southerners still view Democrats as the party of the working class. When asked which party represents the interests of working people, a majority of respondents in all income groups below $100,000 cite the Democrats (see figure 1.4.).

The important group politically is the lower-middle class ($20,000–$50,000). If whites in this income group remain with the Republican Party (see figure 1.4), Democrats will have difficulties putting together a biracial economic coalition. The policy consequences are important because Republicans who advocate less government will not see a major role for government intervention in confronting economic inequality.

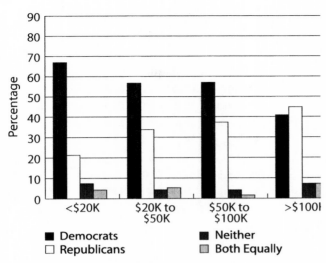

Figure 1.4. Bar chart of income group responses to the question, "Which political party better represents the interests of working people?" Survey of Southern Voters, 2004, Public Opinion Research Laboratory at the University of North Florida, $N =$ 803.

Table 1.8. State Populations Below Poverty Line and Their National Rank

State	% Below poverty line	National rank
Arkansas	18.0%	1
Mississippi	17.6%	3
Louisiana	17.0%	4
Texas	15.3%	6
Alabama	14.6%	8
Tennessee	14.2%	9
South Carolina	13.5%	12
North Carolina	13.1%	14
Florida	12.1%	17
Georgia	12.1%	17
Virginia	8.7%	39
USA	12.4%	

Source: 2000 U.S. Census.

Note: A family of three with an income below $13,470 is considered below the poverty line. Individuals with an income below $8,959 are considered in poverty.

These policies have not hurt Republicans among blue-collar whites. Thus, Republican officeholders have little incentive to revise their policies. Democrats have to try to focus the attention of white working-class conservatives on economic issues (Frank 2004). As Republicans gain even more strength in state-level positions in the South, their policies of low taxation may aid economic growth, but do not address economic inequality. Yet, Democrats do not seem to have an answer to provide governmental assistance to address the economic challenges of the region.

These regionwide data suggest that the fundamental realignment of Southern politics may have important impacts on how the South is governed and how the region confronts the legacy issues of racial differences and economic hardship. Republican leadership may have important effects on Southern society and its politics. To examine these phenomena more intensely, the next chapter presents a case study of a Southern city, Jacksonville, Florida.

The Case Study

Jacksonville, Florida

A city in Florida may seem an unusual choice for a case study of Southern politics. When many Americans think of Florida, the beaches of Miami, Disney World, hurricanes, and the disputed 2000 presidential election come to mind. Yet, a main reason why the controversy of the 2000 election occurred is that southeast Florida has a Democratic tilt and Northern Florida, which was once part of the "Democratic Solid South," now leans heavily Republican. The part of the state that covers the Panhandle and the northeastern shore has a political history resembling that of other regions in the South. The city of Jacksonville was occupied three times by Union forces during the Civil War, and Abraham Lincoln was burned in effigy at the start of the war in a nearby town (Martin 1972). A Confederate war memorial stands tall in a plaza in front of Jacksonville City Hall. Northern Florida has a long history that has little to do with the international flavor of South Florida or the tourist-dominated economy of Central Florida.

The largest city in Florida, Jacksonville is located in northeast Florida near the Georgia border (map 1). The city is consolidated with Duval County to create one of the largest land-mass cities in the United States. The county is varied with the western part of the county having longtime agricultural roots, while the central part of the county is a defined urban area. Southern and eastern Jacksonville are the newer part of the city and resemble the suburbs of many metropolitan areas. The eastern part of the county runs right to the Atlantic Ocean. Per capita annual income is near $33,000. The racial makeup of the county is 64% white, 28% black, and 8% other (Jacksonville Community Council Inc. 2005).

Jacksonville is a coastal city that depends on shipping, the military, banking, real estate, and construction for most of its job opportunities. The downtown is separated by a large river that serves as an economic and environmental asset. According to the 2004 Census update, the population of Jacksonville is nearly 840,474, with a constant population growth rate

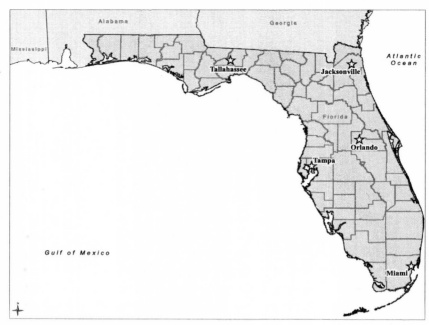

Map 1. Florida's Major Cities.

of 1–2% annually over the last two decades (northeast Florida as whole is home to more than 1.2 million people). Unlike some cities in South Florida that have larger older populations, more than one-quarter (26%) of Jacksonville residents are under age 25 (Jacksonville Community Council Inc. 2005). With its service-oriented economy and growing population, Jacksonville has been labeled an example of the New South. This category includes Southern counties that are "diverse urbanized counties with a high rate of population growth" (Aistrup 1996). In short, Jacksonville has an Old South history with a New South economy.

Why a Case Study?

When choosing to feature a case study, an author must address two questions: 1) Why use a case study?; and 2) Why use this particular case study? As mentioned in chapter 1, important scholars in Southern politics have used a variety of approaches to study politics in the South. Black and Black (1987) and Scher (1997), among others, have focused on the entire region in their important books. The crucial works of Key (1949), Harvard (1952), and Bullock and Rozell (2003) have used a state-by-state approach. While several studies involving Southern cities were done in the civil rights era of the 1960s (Keech 1968; Clubock et al. 1964), there have been very few recent studies focusing on political change in the urban and suburban areas of the South (Button 1989). Moreover, most studies of Southern politics concentrate on a single factor, such as the economy or race, to explain Southern political change. In contrast, this work examines three major factors in Southern politics (race, religion, and economic change) in one study. The advantage of a case-study approach is that a researcher can learn "about a complex instance, based on comprehensive understanding of that instance obtained by extensive description and analysis . . . taken as a whole and in context" (U.S. Government Accounting Office 1990, 14). The complexity of examining these social phenomena simultaneously is greatly aided by examination of one area because the entire context of the political unit can be analyzed.

Why This Case Study?

The following are four reasons to use Jacksonville/Duval County as a case study of Southern politics.

Southern Historical Relevance

The definition used in this study to describe the South is the 11-state South that seceded from the Union during the Civil War. Thus, a case study of Southern politics should reflect an area that has a Southern history with connections to the Civil War and its long impact on race relations and the economy. Jacksonville meets this criterion because the city, along with the rest of Florida, favored the Confederate cause. The city was occupied three times by Union forces that were trying to control sea access to the city. These occupations emptied the city of its residents. A Union soldier remarked, "Jacksonville is or was a very pretty place—but War has ravished it. It is made desolate and lonely" (Martin 1972, 56). After the war, Reconstruction also impacted the city as nine African Americans were elected to the city council during the 1870s and 1880s. Segregation, racial violence, the civil rights movement, and its accompanying white backlash all occurred in Jacksonville. These issues and events will be examined in more detail in chapter 3.

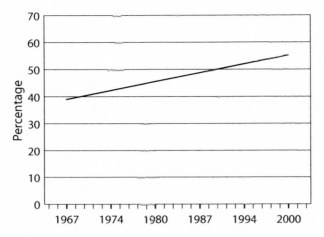

Figure 2.1. Line graph of trend analysis of Republican votes in major elections in Duval County, Florida, from 1967 to 2000. Major elections included presidential, gubernatorial, and mayoral elections. Data provided by the Supervisor of Elections Office in Duval County.

Rise of the Republican Party

In order to examine the impact of partisan change in the South, change must be evident. As seen in Figure 2.1, Republicans have made tremendous gains over the last forty years. Only 5% of Jacksonville residents were registered as Republicans in the mid-1960s. By 2005, 37% of Jacksonville residents were registered Republicans. Meanwhile, Democrats lost nearly 50% of the market share, declining from 95% of registered voters in 1965 to 46% in 2004. With many conservative Democrats voting Republican by the end of the 1990s, Republicans dominated presidential, senatorial, and mayoral races, as the mean trend line in Figure 2.1 demonstrates.

George W. Bush won a decisive victory in the disputed Florida 2000 presidential election in Duval County with 58% of the vote. His brother, former Florida governor Jeb Bush, also won Duval County by large margins in 1998 and 2002. In 1995, John Delaney was elected the first Republican mayor of Jacksonville since Reconstruction. His tenure helped solidify Republican dominance on the local level, and his successor is also a Republican. As of this writing, no white Democrat holds any citywide office, state legislative seat, or Congressional seat in Jacksonville, a statistic that completely reverses the trends of most of the twentieth century.[1]

Consolidation

The joining together of the city and county under consolidation in 1968 launched a period of rapid change and economic growth for Jacksonville. The old Jacksonville city government of the 1950s and 1960s had failed in almost every part of governance. Mayor Haydon Burns led a revitalization of the city core, but the myriad number of commissions and elected officials in Jacksonville government brought about corruption and duplication (Crooks 2004). The most obvious indicator of the failure of Jacksonville's government was that this Florida coastal city was actually losing population in the 1960s. Jacksonville was following the pattern of other American cities, with its white population fleeing to the suburbs outside the governance of the central city. Business leaders in Jacksonville responded to the governance crisis by proposing the merger of the city and the rest of Duval County.[2] The consolidation was approved by Jacksonville residents throughout the city and included support from some, but not all, of the African American precincts. The consolidated city provided economic opportunities with a larger population.

Consolidation provides the opportunity to study political trends at the local level without artificial lines separating parts of the county by municipalities. Moreover, the period of consolidation of 1969–present provides the researcher with a time range that coincides with end of the civil rights period and the rise of the Republican Party in the region. With a central city core and outlying suburbs under one consolidated government, Jacksonville's local politics reflects the politics of larger geographical entities. Whites and African Americans are compelled to interact with each other politically in this setting. Rural, urban, and suburban neighborhoods are all together in one political arena. Focusing on one political unit also allows the researcher to analyze voting behavior for offices from the presidency all the way down to the local level.

Finally, studying consolidated Jacksonville showcases both the challenges of the inner city and the growth issues of the suburbs. The inclusion of suburbs is crucial for a study of Southern politics because these new suburbs are where Republicans have made tremendous gains (Black and Black 2000). The suburbs in the South have produced Newt Gingrich, Tom Delay, Bill Frist, and other Republican conservative leaders.

Table 2.1. Demographic Characteristics of Respondents from Jacksonville, Florida, and the South

	Jacksonville (N = 925–948)[a]	Southern (N = 793–803)[a]
Lived in South when 6	59.4%	64.2%
Native Southerner	23.7%	48.9%
White respondent	71.2%	79.7%
Black respondent	22.4%	14.2%
Hispanic/Latino respondent	3.8%	5.0%
18–30	14.6%	10.4%
31–50	40.7%	44.1%
Older than 50	44.7%	45.5%
Less than $20K	9.3%	13.6%
$20K to $50K	32.3%	31.7%
$50K to $100K	39.3%	36.4%
More than $100K	19.1%	18.4%
Grade school	2.8%	3.4%
High school graduate	20.2%	19.4%
Some college	31.1%	30.0%
College or more	45.9%	47.2%
Democrat identification	34.2%	35.9%
Republican identification	47.8%	35.9%
Protestant	59.4%	61.6%
Catholic	16.3%	14.8%
Jewish	1.6%	2.2%
Other	10.8%	16.3%
None	10.1%	4.0%

Source: Survey of Southern Voters and Jacksonville Voters, 2004–2005. Public Opinion Research Laboratory, University of North Florida.

Note: Lived in South when 6, Native Southerner, White respondent, Republican identification significant at $P \leq .05$ Chi^2 statistic.

[a] Sample size differs depending on the question.

Representativeness of the Study

If a case study can match the characteristics of its larger population, it is much more useful and more generalizable. No one case study can capture all the variations of Southern politics. Each of the 11 Southern states has its own unique characteristics that cannot be duplicated in one study. Yet, a valid case study should be similar to the larger region. With a unique research design, this study can demonstrate the similarities and the differences between the individual case (Jacksonville) and the overall region (the South).

Table 2.2. Comparison of Selected Political Issues for Respondents in Jacksonville and in the South

	Jacksonville (N = 925–948)[a]	Southern (N = 794–803)[a]
Consider yourself a Southerner	70.1%	74.7%
Blacks experience daily discrimination	57.2%	56.9%
Affirmative action is needed	38.8%	34.6%
Concerned about declining morals	87.7%	89.8%
Oppose gay marriage	67.8%	69.9%
Pro-life	49.8%	50.0%
Gov't should protect economy vs. environment	39.7%	45.8%
Republican party helps middle class more	46.3%	36.7%
Support war in Iraq	57.6%	57.3%
Oppose war in Iraq	40.1%	39.4%
1–100 George W. Bush (mean)	58.85	57.62
1–100 Bill Clinton (mean)	47.37	43.43
1–100 Ronald Reagan (mean)	71.40	64.33

Source: Survey of Southern Voters and Jacksonville Voters. Public Opinion Research Lab, University of North Florida.
Note: Daily discrimination and Republican Party helps the middle class more significant at P ≤. 05 chi^2 statistic.

This design includes the administration of random-digit-dialing methodology of a 50-question survey to 803 voters in the 11 Southern states in February 2004. The sample was stratified to reflect the population in each state. A questionnaire was developed that focused on questions concerning race relations, religious attitudes, and economic attitudes. The same questionnaire was then administered to more than 1,000 Jacksonville voters in 2004/2005.[3] Thus, the responses of Southern voters and Jacksonville voters can be compared. Table 2.1 compares the demographics of the two samples. Among the demographics, only native status, racial background, and voter registration have statistically significant differences. While these categories differ, most of the differences are not large. The exception is the percentage of native Southerners in the two units. However, when longtime Southerners are included, a different picture emerges. When we add those Southerners who have been in the South since they were six years old, the differences shrink dramatically.

Jacksonville has more new Southerners, more Republicans, and more African Americans than does the entire South. Yet, these differences portend the South of the future. The South as a region is increasing in all three categories. The rise of the Republican Party is well documented. Moreover, African Americans are moving back to the South in greater numbers, reversing the effects of the Great Migration (Frey 1998) of the early twentieth century. Also, the phenomenal population growth that the South continues to experience will greatly increase the number of non-natives in the region. The case study of Jacksonville reflects all of these trends.

In terms of attitudes, the two units show tremendous similarity. Identification as a Southerner shows little difference. In a sampling of questions on political issues, few divisions emerge. Both residents of Jacksonville and Southerners recognize that racial discrimination exists, but neither supports affirmative action. Respondents in both geographic areas are concerned about morals in the nation and strongly oppose gay marriage. Support for the war in Iraq in 2004 was almost identical. Thermometer opinion scores for President George W. Bush are almost the same, while both President Clinton and President Reagan score slightly better in Jacksonville than in the South as a whole.

As stated above, no single study could completely replicate the South as a whole. Yet, the data reveal that the city of Jacksonville has a population that is growing in Republicans, African Americans, and non-Southerners. Residents' attitudes are similar to those of Southerners in general. These factors are good indicators that a study of the political trends of Jacksonville/Duval County can give the reader insights into what is happening in the region as a whole.

Resegregation of Southern Politics

During the hotly disputed 2004 presidential election, Florida Democrats sought revenge for the 2000 election controversy. In Duval County alone more than 27,000 ballots in the 2000 presidential race were not tabulated due to overvoting and undervoting. While the national media gave less attention to Jacksonville than to other cities in Florida, it was probably in Jacksonville that Al Gore lost the 2000 election in Florida. In almost one out of ten ballots cast in Jacksonville, the presidential vote was not tabulated.

Accordingly, in the fall of 2004, prior to the next presidential election, a group comprised of U.S. House Representative Corrine Brown, an African American Democrat from Jacksonville, local ministers, and representatives from the Southern Christian Leadership Conference stood before the Duval County supervisor of elections and demanded attention. These leaders wanted the local Republican supervisor of elections to open additional early-voting sites in Duval County. Political activist Jesse Jackson rushed to the city to join the protest as well.

Early voting allowed voters to cast their ballots in person two weeks before Election Day. Early voting was being pushed especially hard in African American precincts in Jacksonville. Over the previous 30 years, Jacksonville had become a Republican stronghold on the presidential level, and Democrats were seeking to cut the margin in Jacksonville and win the state with an overwhelming advantage in South Florida. Generally, more Republicans voted by absentee and more African American Democrats voted by early voting. In Florida, county supervisor of elections (SOE) officials gain office by partisan elections. In Duval County, the Republican assistant supervisor of elections steadfastly refused to open more sites and ended the discussion in front of the cameras. Black leaders called the assistant SOE director "arrogant" (DeCamp 2004). A casual observer of this racially charged scene—black leaders being refused service by a white supervisor of elections—might easily have thought that the year was 1964, not 2004. Black

Figure 3.1. Rev. Jesse Jackson, *left*, talks with Duval County Assistant Supervisor of Elections Dick Carlberg, *right*, about opening additional early-voting sites in October 2004. (Photo reproduced by permission of the *Florida Times Union*.)

leaders saw this episode as a continuation of unfair treatment by election officials; Republicans saw it as a publicity stunt.

The fact that black leaders and white election officials were confronting each other in the election of 2004 indicates the lasting potency of race relations in Southern politics. Facts on the ground have changed dramatically since 1964. African Americans vote in the nearly the same proportion to whites in Duval County. Six African Americans now serve on the city council. A black sheriff was elected twice in the 1990s. Yet the example at the SOE office shows that race still plays a major role in elections in Duval County. African Americans are increasingly becoming a majority group in a minority party while white voters dominate the Republican Party. This essential dynamic is a central element of the politics of the county and the region. Having two major political parties separated along racial lines is a major consequence of Republican ascendancy to power. Before examining the impacts of this partisan and racial separation, it is important to ask why race is still paramount in the social and political lives of Southerners.

Why Should Race Matter?

After the successes of the civil rights movement regarding voting, accommodations, and access to educational facilities, why is race such an important factor in Southern politics? In the example of our case study, two primary reasons are paramount. The historical record of race relations from the Civil War (1865) through the civil rights period (1965) shows a community separated by race. These historical events will take more than one generation to overcome. Secondly, the relative social inequality that still exists between whites and blacks in the county fosters tension and a lack of trust between whites and blacks. These factors, combined with the increasing separation of the races into two different political parties, create a formidable divide.

History

As stated previously, a case study of Southern politics should include Southern history. As it does in other parts of the South, the history of race relations in Jacksonville heavily impacts the politics of today. This history has been inconsistent and mixed, with relations between whites and blacks varying tremendously over the years. During certain periods, Jacksonville has been seen as a good place for African Americans to live; during other periods, the city has experienced problems identical to those found in Mississippi, Alabama, and South Carolina.

The city was founded in 1821, with African Americans being a significant part of the population. When the city was occupied in the Civil War, hundreds of black Union soldiers entered the city and offered a new perspective to native blacks (Bartley 2000). During the Reconstruction period, Jacksonville was seen as a place of hope for blacks. The seaport offered economic prospects, and Reconstruction laws offered political opportunity. Seven blacks were elected to the city council between 1868 and 1888. In contrast with freed slaves in other Southern cities, African Americans in Jacksonville actually increased their political fortunes in 1890s. A yellow fever epidemic caused thousands of white citizens to leave the city. This white flight allowed African Americans to outnumber whites. Black citizens soon took advantage of their numerical superiority by electing five African Americans to the city council. White Democrats believed that black citizens were trying to take over the city. The Florida State Legislature cancelled the results of the elections and put in place a white city council, which, in turn, elected a white mayor in 1893 (Bartley 2000).

Reductions in black political power would happen over and over again in Jacksonville's history. Each time black political power rose, white Democrats would find legal and economic ways to reduce this power. African Americans again made political gains in the 1899 elections. Yet, through a combination of purging African Americans from voting lists, poll taxes, and unusual voting practices, black political influence in the city almost disappeared by 1910 (Bartley 2000). Leading the backlash were the Redeemers, white Democrats who wanted to see a return of white supremacy after the Civil War. While it took a bit longer in Jacksonville than it did in other places in the South, the Redeemers won. The victory of the Redeemers in the early part the twentieth century presented a particularly cruel irony in Duval County. Blacks were now excluded from politics in a city where they made up the majority.

After World War I, black soldiers returned home to the United States and sought their constitutional rights. With the passage of the Nineteenth Amendment in 1920, African American women also started to demand the right to vote. Thus, the 1920 election became a litmus test for black voting rights. Most African Americans were Republicans at this time in Jacksonville, and the Democratic Party establishment fought their participation. Black leaders formed Republican political clubs to increase the political activity of blacks. The Ku Klux Klan and other elements tried to intimidate potential black voters throughout Florida in the 1920 presidential election. The Klan marched in Jacksonville immediately before the election of 1920 as a warning to blacks not to vote. Election officials in Jacksonville intentionally limited the number of precincts in African American areas of the city on Election Day to further reduce the black vote. Many blacks who stood on line were not allowed to vote before the polls closed (Ortiz 2005).

Due to a northern migration of blacks and an overall increase in population, whites again became a majority of the residents in the 1920s and white political power reasserted its dominance. Jim Crow laws and social mores were in full force in Jacksonville during the first half of the twentieth century. African American influence was generally confined to black-owned businesses and churches. The Afro-American Insurance Company, founded by A. L. Lewis in the early 1900s, became one of the most successful African American businesses in the nation, setting a standard for other black enterprises to emulate. The Lavilla community in downtown Jacksonville provided a social and economic center for blacks in the city (Crooks 2004).

Just as in World War I, the returning wave of African American soldiers after World War II led to a rise in black political activism in the city.

Even though they were heavily discouraged by the local Democratic Party, thousands of blacks registered to vote in the late 1940s (Bartley 2000). This registration success led to a surprising result: the election of an African American justice of the peace in 1956. Electing a black to any office was a considerable achievement. Yet, it would be an achievement that would not last. The local Democratic executive committee nullified the election results and sued to put its own white candidate in office. This rejection set the stage for a long and sustained political movement among Jacksonville's black community (Bartley 2000).

The civil rights period in Jacksonville was marked in 1960 by an attack on black protestors known as "Ax Handle" Sunday, during which local police allowed Ku Klux Klan members and other angry whites to beat black protestors with ax handles. Scholar Abel Bartley viewed this attack as one of the worst moments for African Americans in the city. The police department's failure to protect African Americans showed again how important it was for blacks to be part of the political process. A second major incident occurred in March 1964 when a week of violence broke out following the arrest of black school children who supported the boycott of segregated businesses downtown (Crooks 2004). While the Civil Rights Act was being debated in Washington, Jacksonville became another example of a city experiencing race riots. Black teenagers were arrested for throwing homemade bombs into buildings and committing other acts of vandalism. An African American woman, Johnnie Mae Chapelle, was randomly gunned down on the street by a white man looking to kill a black person.[1] Mayor Haydon Burns, who had won the black vote in most elections, directly refused to push desegregation. The mayor appointed a community relations committee to mediate the crisis, but many black leaders refused to take part if desegregation was not the goal of the group (*Florida Times-Union* 1964, A1).

Inequality of Status

While political progress was slow for African Americans after Jim Crow laws were passed in the early 1900s, social progress was even more elusive. On almost every social indicator, blacks were greatly separated from whites. After World War II, a local group of agencies called the Council of Social Agencies put together a comprehensive report on the state of blacks in Jacksonville in 1945. In this report, titled *Jacksonville Looks at Its Negro Community*, several social agencies in the city described the relative status of blacks in regards to health, job opportunities, education, and housing.

The report's findings painted a devastating portrait of the status of blacks in Jacksonville. Twenty years before Daniel Patrick Moynihan declared that there were two societies in the United States, one black and one white (Moynihan 1996), the Jacksonville report anticipated those conclusions. In terms of health, blacks had a death rate that was 50% higher than whites in the late 1940s. For African Americans, the infant mortality rate was an alarming 76 deaths for every 1,000 births (twice the rate of whites). Tuberculosis was the leading cause of death among blacks. Access to health care was a serious problem. Since medical facilities were segregated, only one hospital in the city would treat blacks. There were only 10 black doctors to care for over 68,000 black residents. The hospital lacked the latest medical advances and was understaffed. Over a four-year period, 130 blacks were murdered in the city, most by other African Americans, while only nine whites were murdered during the same period.

Sanitation was another major problem for blacks in the city. Many streets in the black community were unpaved, and sewer service was not available to thousands of black residents. The report cited housing for blacks as an "acute" problem. Many blacks lived in old structures with no solid foundations (Council of Social Agencies 1945).

Economic opportunity also was difficult for black members of the segregated community. Whites dominated the professional job sector, while most blacks were relegated to domestic work and laborer status. Not surprisingly, lack of access to quality education and substandard educational facilities were major impediments for blacks during this time. The black segregated schools had little equipment and paid their teachers much less than did white schools in the community. The report said that the conditions of the black schools were poor and that "many of the schools are still dependent upon outside toilet facilities" (Council of Social Agencies 1945, 45). We need to compare these earlier conditions with those at the beginning of the 21st century in order to examine current racial dynamics in the city.

The economy of the city and the region has improved dramatically since the 1960s. This growth will be examined in chapter 5. The city of Jacksonville became a major economic force in the South with a diversified economy. The standard of living rose substantially in the city and the region. With this economic success, the gap between African Americans and whites should have narrowed. Yet, the inequality of status has persisted.

The Jacksonville Community Council Inc., a local citizens' study group, produced an updated look at race relations in the community in 2004. They measured many of the same policy areas examined by the 1945 report. The 2004 report showed that despite the city's overall economic and social progress since the 1960s, serious differences remain between many blacks and white residents when social indicators are examined. The standard of living for most Jacksonville residents has improved dramatically since the 1940s, but the rise in the standard of living has not occurred proportionately.

In regard to health and medical care, disparities between blacks and whites are actually increasing. The infant mortality rate among blacks is almost three times that of white citizens. Nearly a quarter of all African American babies are born to mothers without a high school education. In a city that is 27% African American, only 5% of the doctors are black. In terms of perceptions, more than half of blacks surveyed said that white citizens have better access to health care than do blacks (Jacksonville Community Council Inc. 2005).

Economic progress for blacks has varied tremendously among income groups. Jacksonville's black middle and upper income classes have expanded dramatically. Almost one in five black families makes over $60,000 a year. The city has thousands of black professionals who have succeeded socially and economically. Despite these advances, tremendous economic disparities remain. Nearly half of all black families in the community have a family income below $30,000 (175% of the poverty line), while 29% of white families are in the same category. Only 4% of the CEOs in Jacksonville are black. Moreover, no blacks are head of any of the 50 fastest-growing companies in the region. In math and reading, the areas of education that are central to economic advancement, black students score at least 25% below white students at every grade level, K-12. The black graduation rate from high school is 18% lower than the white graduation rate (Jacksonville Community Council Inc. 2005).

These indicators reveal a central fact about the relative position of whites and blacks in Jacksonville. Despite tremendous political progress since the civil rights movement of the 1960s and some marked economic gains, a large underclass remains in the city and this underclass is disproportionately black. While median family income has risen in Jacksonville since the 1960s, the differences between whites and blacks on many social indicators are *increasing* 40 years after the civil rights movement.

These stark realities occur in a political environment where serious differences of opinion exist as to whether government should play a large role in addressing these disparities. Many whites believe that African Americans who are in difficult circumstances are responsible for those circumstances. In a 2000 Jacksonville University survey, 85% of white respondents said they believed that a black applicant would have an equal chance of getting a job as would a white applicant if he or she were qualified (Jacksonville Community Council Incorporated 2005).

Many African Americans believe that present and historical discrimination play a large role in difficulties that some in the black community are facing. Additionally, many blacks in the community feel that the local sheriff's office unfairly targets minorities. Simply put, race still matters in politics in Jacksonville and in the South because race matters in everything else in the South. The combination of different histories and different economic positions permeates the political atmosphere and makes it almost inevitable that most whites and most blacks are split into two political parties. This partisan split provided new political choices for Jacksonville voters, but it also created a political dynamic in which racial and economic disparities are difficult to address. This partisan split and its consequences are examined below.

1964: The Partisan Split Begins

The year 1964 proved a pivotal moment for strong black identification with the Democratic Party. Thirty years earlier, the New Deal had provided the first pull to the Democratic Party for blacks who could vote. The 1960s would be another turning point. President Johnson's leadership on civil rights contrasted sharply with Republican presidential candidate Barry Goldwater's stance on state's rights. White residents in Jacksonville who had seen the city deteriorate into racial violence during 1964 came out strongly for Barry Goldwater in the 1964 election. African American voters in Jacksonville rallied behind Johnson. As in other parts of the South, Goldwater won a majority of the votes in the city. This election was an important development. Until 1964, white Democrats in Jacksonville had been faithful members of the Democratic Solid South. The city voted for Harry Truman in 1948 despite the presence of the Dixiecrat Strom Thurmond on the ballot. While Thurmond got 25% of the vote, he finished third in the city. The 1952 and 1956 campaigns were disasters for Democrats nationally, but in Duval County, liberal Democratic governor Adlai Stevenson won in 1952 and trailed Dwight D. Eisenhower in 1956 by only 300 votes. In 1960, John F. Kennedy, a Catholic Democrat, won by 10% in a city dominated by Southern Protestants.

In contrast, the period of 1964 represented an important shift for white Democrats in Jacksonville. Lyndon Johnson had led the legislative charge for the 1964 Civil Rights Act. This act was the most important civil rights legislation in the nation since Reconstruction. Segregationists thought that the act was the largest intrusion of federal power upon the states since the New Deal. Barry Goldwater won a heated battle between the conservative and moderate wings of the Republican Party to take the nomination in 1964. Earlier, Goldwater had written off the black vote for Republicans. This was a curious strategy considering that since the Civil War, the Republican Party, the party of Lincoln, had been the party of choice for most black Americans. Goldwater said that Republicans needed to focus on white Southerners by going hunting "where the ducks are" (Carter 2000, 218). He boldly said he would carry the fight for "states' rights" on matters concerning integration. Many white Jacksonville Democrats supported Goldwater for two reasons. He voted against the Civil Rights Act of 1964, and they wanted to make a statement about the race riots that had erupted in the city that year. The day prior to the election in 1964, the lead headline in the local newspaper read, "Arizonan Hits Rights Act" (*Florida Times-Union* 1964, A1). Goldwater had traveled to Columbia, South Carolina, and declared before a crowd of Confederate flag-waving supporters that the Civil Rights Act was unconstitutional. His speech, carried on television across the South, was the last image many Southerners had of Goldwater before the election.

Goldwater's national campaign was a disaster because he talked recklessly about nuclear weapons. Yet white Southerners heard his call. The local newspaper reported the next day that Goldwater had won in North Florida solely due to his opposition to civil rights: "In North Florida, an area closely tied to the neighboring Old South states of Georgia and Alabama, Democrats swung to Goldwater simply because of his vote against the Civil Rights Bill. Here the issue was black and white" (*Florida Times-Union* 1964, A3).

In 1968, segregationist George Wallace took up the cause of the disenchanted Southern white voter with his independent campaign for President. On cue, Wallace talked about law and order. This emphasis was a thinly veiled racial appeal since the race riots of 1966–1968 had captured the nation's attention. In addition, the civil rights movement was becoming more confrontational after 1965. The black nationalist movement became a provocative alternative to the traditional civil rights leadership of Martin Luther King Jr. Wallace was the ideal candidate to take up the white Southern cause. While he still appeared with segregationists groups like the White Citizens Councils, his campaign did not focus only on race. He appealed to the white working class by talking about misguided Washington, D.C., elites and making fun of long-haired Vietnam War protestors. Wallace won a plurality of the votes for president in 1968 in Jacksonville while also winning five Southern states.

With Goldwater representing Republicans in 1964 and Wallace running as an independent in 1968, the Democratic Party was the only real choice for African Americans in Duval County. While African Americans had been repelled by local Democrats for generations, the New Deal and the civil rights movement lured blacks to the Democratic Party. The years 1964 and 1968 ushered in a new racial divide in local politics: African American citizens registered and remained Democrats, and white citizens began to look at other options.

On the local level, consolidation of Duval County and the city of Jacksonville fundamentally changed the city and its politics. The city consolidated with the entire county in the late 1960s. This was an important political development for local African Americans. They faced the choice of voting for economic opportunities versus gaining political power. By the mid-1960s, African Americans made up more than 40% of the city's population. With the passage of the Civil Rights Act of 1964 and the Voting Rights Act of 1965, blacks began to register and vote in greater numbers. With these trends, it was predicted that blacks would soon occupy many of the city's elected positions if the city remained the same. Yet the state of the city's government was so poor that several African American leaders urged their fellow black citizens to support consolidation. The city and county were governed by a myriad of commissions and boards. Businesses found it difficult to obtain permits and understand the different regulations that were required by the various government boards. Since most local taxes were paid by property taxes, the inner core of the city did not provide enough revenue to provide important services. African American leadership was split on whether to support consolidation, but most blacks voted for consolidation. Table 3.1 shows that the percentage of African American Democrats went from 38% of registered voters in 1965 to 22% in the expanded city in 1975. By adding the surrounding growing suburbs to the city/county, Jacksonville's racial dynamics changed forever. The nearly 50% decline in the proportion of African American voters in Jacksonville reshaped politics in the region. Urban scholar Abel Bartley brilliantly summed up the effects of consolidation in Jacksonville, remarking that black voters of the time "had to choose between sharing power in an economically strong White city or dominating a bankrupt Black community" (Bartley 2000).

Table 3.1. Number and Percentage of Total Registered Voters in Duval County, Florida

	1965[a]		1975		1985		1995		2005	
White Dems.	46,556	56%	140,111	61%	150,752	48%	126,531	36%	107,551	21%
Black Dems.	31,456	38%	51,456	22%	76,908	25%	74,715	25%	116,564	23%
White GOP	2,680	3%	31,683	14%	66,261	21%	113,296	33%	190,706	33%
Black GOP	1,330	2%	1,191	.1%	1,793	.1%	3,446	.1%	5,926	1%
Total Dems.	78,112	95%	191,567	83%	227,660	73%	203,305	59%	238,264	46%
Total GOP	4,010	5%	32,874	14%	68,054	21%	119,235	34%	190,111	37%
Total Others	465	0%	6,435	3%	16,030	5%	23,812	7%	86,827	17%

Source: Supervisor of Elections Office, Duval County, Florida.

Note: [a] 1965 was before city-county consolidation. 2002 numbers reflect new registration procedures under the Federal Motor Voter Act.

Starting in 1972, Jacksonville assumed a new political identity: that of an area leaning Republican at the presidential level and solidly Democratic at the local level. The Republican Southern strategy of trying to separate white conservatives from the Democratic Party began in full force. In 1972, the Democratic Party shifted to the left by nominating George McGovern. This nomination created an opening for Republicans in the South. Moreover, the assassination attempt on George Wallace's life left white conservatives in northeast Florida with only one place to go—Richard Nixon, and he received an astounding 68% of the vote in Duval County in 1972.

However, Watergate and Jimmy Carter combined to solidify the Democratic Party in northeast Florida. Carter's credentials as a born-again Baptist, along with his pledge to return integrity to the Oval Office after the Watergate scandal, played well in the conservative South. Carter's emphasis on faith also endeared him in North Florida to white conservative churches that were becoming more active in the political process. Carter won Duval County and became the last Democratic presidential candidate to win a majority in Jacksonville. Locally, a former circuit judge, Democrat Hans Tanzler, dominated the political scene. He ran without Republican opposition in 1971 and won a convincing re-election bid in 1975. Carter and Tan-

Figure 3.2. Republican candidate Ronald Reagan visiting Jacksonville during the 1980 presidential campaign. (Photo reproduced by permission of the *Florida Times Union*.)

zler managed to halt Republican advancement in northeast Florida in the mid-1970s (Corrigan 2000).

This was an important opportunity for both national and local Democrats. For the first time since the civil rights period, Carter had brought white and black Democrats together under one presidential banner. If Southern Democrats could maintain a biracial coalition, they could dominate politics in the region. Yet, the difficulties of the one-term Carter presidency opened the door for a conservative Republican to stake his claim to the white Southern vote. In the 1980 presidential election, Democrats missed the opportunity to forge a new Democratic Party in the South. From 1980 onward, partisan differences and racial differences would nearly become one and the same.

Reagan's presence on the Republican ticket in 1980 energized Republicans in the South, including northeast Florida. With independent John Anderson on the ballot in 1980, Reagan beat Southerner Jimmy Carter in Jacksonville. This victory was significant because Reagan accelerated the rise of Republicans in the region. In fact, the Reagan victory may have accelerated a shift toward Republicans in the South *below* the presidential level.

Table 3.2. Thermometer Scale of Current and Past Presidents among Whites and Blacks in Jacksonville

	Whites		Blacks	
	Mean	St. Dev.	Mean	St. Dev.
George W. Bush	67.34[a]	33.238	34.60[d]	31.053
Bill Clinton	35.78[b]	32.653	81.96[e]	22.890
Ronald Reagan	72.13[c]	25.364	51.50[f]	30.745

Source: Survey of Jacksonville Voters, 2004–2005. Public Opinion Research Laboratory, University of North Florida.

Notes: [a] $N = 656$
[b] $N = 656$
[c] $N = 648$
[d] $N = 200$
[e] $N = 202$
[f] $N = 201$

Republican strategists were becoming increasingly frustrated at being competitive on the presidential level in the South but not on other levels. The Reagan victory in 1980 and the accompanying takeover of the U.S. Senate by Republicans inspired a new generation of conservative Southerners to run for Congress, state legislatures, and local offices under the Republican banner. Table 3.2 shows the enduring popularity of Reagan among whites in Jacksonville on a scale of 1–100.

Moreover, Republican success in presidential and senatorial races led to Republican success in other offices. This success exacerbated the racial divide in Jacksonville politics because nearly every winning Republican was a former white Democrat. Reagan's push to get government off the backs of Americans reminded African Americans of other politicians like Strom Thurmond and Barry Goldwater who had preached "states' rights."

The data in table 3.3 reveal a pattern of top-down Republicanism. The presidential, senatorial, and gubernatorial levels (rows 1–3) show that throughout the period examined, Republican candidates were competitive. However, in the 1990s, Republican candidates for most of these offices consistently received a majority or a plurality of the vote in Duval County. Until Jeb Bush won the Florida governorship in 1998, Florida had elected only one Republican governor since 1966.

As many scholars have noted, Democrats have not surrendered all Southern political offices. Until the 1990s, the barriers for Republican candidates on the congressional (U.S. House of Representatives) and state legislative levels were difficult to overcome. A coalition of conservative white Democrats and black Democrats kept Democratic congressman Charles Bennett in office in Florida's Third Congressional District in Jacksonville. Until 1992, the district covered most of the county, and Bennett was able to emphasize his military knowledge and his seat on the House Armed Services Committee to attract conservatives while offering consistent support for civil rights issues to attract black voters. From 1968 to his retirement in 1992, Bennett had no serious challengers. The combined advantages of the incumbency and the black-white coalition made Duval County a classic example of split-level realignment until the late 1980s and early 1990s (Bolce, De Maio, and Muzzio 1992).

Due to pressure to create minority-access districts to increase minority participation in Congress (Scher 1997), most of Jacksonville was split into two congressional districts in the early 1990s. The Fourth Congressional District covers most of Jacksonville, especially the suburban areas, along with the coastal and rural areas of five adjacent counties. During the 1990s this district was represented by Republican Tillie Fowler, who specialized in military affairs. The district now is overwhelmingly white (85%) and has a solid Republican majority of registered voters. The district is now so secure

Table 3.3. Republican Advancement Selected Years, 1968-2004, in Duval County, Florida

	68	70	71	72	74	75	76	78	80
% of GOP presidential vote	30			68			41		50
% of GOP U.S. Senate vote	54	40			40		35		52
% of GOP gubernatorial vote		49			40			47	
% of GOP U.S. House vote District 3	21				19				22
% of GOP U.S. House vote District 4	Not in Duval	Not in Duval							
% of GOP seats held in state Senate delegation	20	20			0		0	0	0
% of GOP seats held in state House delegation	18	18		22	22		11	22	22
% vote for GOP mayoral nominee			No Nom.			41			

Source: Supervisor of Elections Office, Duval County

for Republicans that no Democrat has made a serious run in the district since 1992.

Florida's Third Congressional District covers a slim section of Jacksonville's downtown and east side, which are heavily black, and then spreads out from the northern part of the state to Central Florida. This district is represented by an African American Democrat, Representative Corrine Brown. Brown's victory in 1992 shows the impact of the redistricting process in the early 1990s. Since African Americans became a numerical force in local politics, white Democrats had tried to appear conservative to white voters and progressive to African American voters. Brown's election put an end to this balancing act. She declared herself a "yellow dog Democrat" (Brown 2004).

This advantage has allowed the Democrats to hold on to the Third Congressional District. Yet, more importantly, Democrats have been drained from other surrounding Congressional districts near Duval County, and Republicans have solid control of these districts. The slim section of Jacksonville in the third district is overwhelmingly African American. State legislative districts and city council districts have followed the same pattern. In effect, the Jacksonville area has been separated into a majority area that re-

83	84	86	87	88	90	91	92	94	95	96	98	99	00	02	03	04
	62			63			49			50			58			59
		43		56			37	73			41		54			56
		49				53		57			59			61		
				22			44	43		39	41		39	41		No Nom.
	35			50	57		58						70	96		96
	0	33		66	66		66	66		66	66		66	66		66
	14	43		43	28		63	63		63	63		75	75		75
25			No Nom.			No Nom.			50			Unopp.			58	

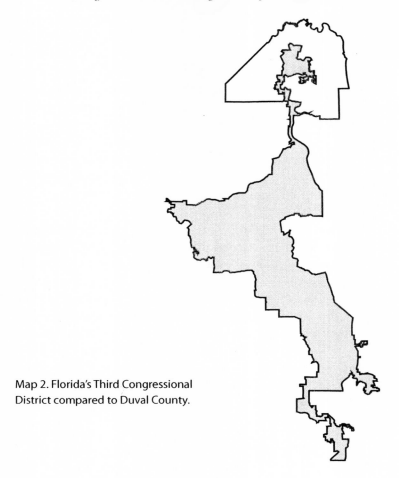

Map 2. Florida's Third Congressional
District compared to Duval County.

flects white conservatives and another smaller area that represents African
American Democrats. The racial separation between the two parties that
began in 1964 has now been codified into law by the redistricting process
at the national, state, and local levels. No longer do most elected officials in
Jacksonville have to balance the interests of white and black residents.

It was not until Jacksonville's 1995 mayoral election that Republicans
fielded a quality candidate for the mayor's office. The incumbent mayor
decided against running for a second term. Two former Democratic mayors moved in to fill the void and announced that they would run. It appeared that, once again, Republicans had no formidable candidate, especially against two experienced Democrats. About three months before the

unitary election in April 1995, the chief of staff to the then-current Democratic mayor announced that he would run for mayor as a Republican. Thus, the first election had two experienced Democratic candidates with a new Republican contender. Republicans hoped that the Democrats would split traditional Democratic support and allow their candidate to make the general election. This scenario is exactly what happened when Republican candidate John Delaney made the second election by gathering 32% of the vote. The two Democratic candidates split their vote 33% to 22%. Moreover, a popular Democratic African American candidate for sheriff also ran in the same election, which brought more Democrats to the polls for the first election.

The former Democratic mayor who made the runoff epitomized traditional Southern Democratic values. He was a white Jacksonville native who had built a coalition of black and white Democrats. The Republican challenger emphasized that he represented a "fresh start" for politics in Jacksonville. He attempted to build a coalition of new residents, who tend to be Republican, with conservative white Democrats (Florida Times Union 1995, A1). The Republican won an extremely close election with 51% of the vote. The former Democratic mayor lost by 3,011 votes out of nearly 160,000 votes cast. This election was a turning point for local Democrats. The city council is now dominated by Republicans. As mentioned above, of the 40 elected positions in the county and city, none is held by a white Democrat. While some black Republicans have had success running for office, most elected Republican officials are white, and most elected Democrats are black. The racial schism between the two parties that first appeared in 1964 had become complete by the beginning of the new century.

Consequences of Combining Racial and Partisan Division

As stated in chapter 1, the central question that this study addresses is, Does the new political reality of Republican dominance in the South matter? The answer on the issue of race is definitively yes. The correlation between partisanship and racial differences creates serious barriers to compromise and coalition building. With the two-party system in the United States, parties act as "linkage" institutions (Maisel 1999). The major parties are supposed to collect many different interests under their respective tents. The two-party system helps to achieve some type of social consensus. While two parties should have different interests and views on issues, consensus exists across the political spectrum on matters such as legitimacy of the Constitution, governmental institutions, and regulated capitalism (Bibby 2000). Yet, now the South has two parties that are generally separated along racial lines. Partisan differences that reflect racial differences exacerbate tensions because racial issues supplant consensus on almost every issue. Mundane issues such as street maintenance, the placement of sewer lines, and the building of parks become immediately controversial because white Republicans generally view these issues one way and black Democrats view them another. Because of partisan trends and the way districts are drawn, elected white Republicans can concentrate on the concerns of white Southerners. Elected African American officials concentrate on the concerns of black citizens. The biracial coalitions of the 1960s and 1970s are vanishing from Southern politics. Thus, public policy concerns are seen as differences that are literally "black" and "white."

Without compromise between the two parties, no serious public policy issues can be addressed successfully. Just as in the South as a whole, the partisan breakdown of Jacksonville residents reflects the racial makeup of the region. For a full examination of the important impacts of the combination of race and partisanship, three groups are profiled: white Republicans, white moderates, and black Democrats. White Republicans and black Democrats need to be compared because they represent the bases of their respective parties. Southern whites who identify themselves as Republican are either transplants to the South who have brought their Republicanism with them or they are native Southerners who have switched parties. White Southern Republicans represent the most conservative partisans in the most conservative region in the country. As Democratic political leaders such as

Table 3.4. With Which Political Party Do You Identify?

	All Whites[a]	White moderates[b]	Blacks[c]
Democratic	21.2%	26.4%	82.9%
Republican	63.7%	52.0%	7.1%
Independent	9.8%	13.1%	4.9%
Other	5.3%	8.4%	5.2%

Source: Survey of Jacksonville Voters, 2004–2005. Public Opinion Research Laboratory, University of North Florida.
Note: Whites vs. Blacks significant at $P \le .05$ chi^2 statistic.
[a] $N = 642$
[b] $N = 244$
[c] $N = 368$

Sam Nunn of Georgia, Fritz Hollings of South Carolina, and Howell Heflin of Alabama have left public life, most white conservative Democrats have left the Democratic Party and voted Republican. Tables 3.4 and 3.5 highlight this trend. Most party switchers are former white Democrats who have turned Republican.

Like white Republicans, black Democrats are the base of their party. Demonstrating an astounding party loyalty, black Democrats make up the most important block of the Democratic Party in most of the South. No Democrat who runs statewide in any Southern state can win without overwhelming support from African American voters. This political power allows blacks to help form the policies and the political strategies of the Democratic Party.

Because white Republicans and black Democrats are so important to their respective parties, party politics automatically become racial politics in many instances. The relative position of these two groups on major issues helps define politics and race relations in the South.

However, throughout Southern history, a third group, white political moderates, has played an important role in brokering race relations in the South. Black and Black (1987) show how moderate segregationists became nonsegregationist as soon as more blacks registered to vote. Martin Luther King Jr. saw white moderates as a key to winning the civil rights movement in the South. Moreover, white Democratic moderates were the most successful political candidates in the South throughout the 1970s and 1980s. They achieved success by building biracial coalitions and representing these coalitions with attention to issues of concern to African Americans (Bullock and Rozell 2003). In sum, white moderates have mediated between blacks and conservative whites through recent Southern history. Accordingly, these self-identified white moderates can represent "tipping points"

Table 3.5. In the Last 20 Years, Have You Switched Political Parties?

	Black Democrats[a]	White Republicans[b]
Yes	3.2%	23.1%
No	96.8%	76.9%

Source: Survey of Jacksonville Voters, 2004–2005. Public Opinion Research Laboratory, University of North Florida.
Note: $P \leq .05$ chi^2 statistic.
[a] $N = 304$
[b] $N = 408$

Table 3.6. Which of the Following Statements Is Closest to Your View about Affirmative Action?

	All Whites[a]	White Republicans[b]	White Moderates[c]	Blacks[d]
Affirmative action is needed	26.6%	18.5%	32.1%	86.5%
Affirmative action is not needed	73.4%	81.5%	67.9%	13.5%

Source: Survey of Jacksonville Voters, 2004–2005. Public Opinion Research Laboratory, University of North Florida.
Note: Blacks vs. Whites significant at P ≤ .05 chi^2 statistic.
[a] $N = 584$
[b] $N = 365$
[c] $N = 219$
[d] $N = 357$

in politics in the South. Moderates include voters from both parties, as well as independents. Independents who wish to register in Florida must do so under the category "No Party Affiliation." Accordingly, only about 10% of Duval County voters are registered as independents. Florida also is a closed primary state, a status that discourages nonpartisan registration. Thus, the term *moderate* is more encompassing. A comparison of white Republicans and African American Democrats can identify these tipping points.

The central differences in opinion between white Republicans and African Americans are twofold: 1) the relative position of blacks in society; and 2) the government's responsibility for doing something about that condition. Figure 3.3 shows the differing perceptions regarding current discrimination.

While a majority of whites believes that African Americans experience discrimination, white Republicans are not convinced. The perceptions of white Republicans stand in complete contrast to those of African Americans, with nearly 90% stating that discrimination exists. While these differences are not surprising, the degree of these differences is wide. If white Republicans and black Democrats hold such starkly different opinions on whether blacks encounter racial discrimination, they will agree on little else regarding race relations. In contrast, a solid majority of white moderates recognizes that discrimination persists against African Americans, and again they appear to be an important swing group on this fundamental idea.

Not surprisingly, attitudes toward a government role in addressing discrimination vary greatly as well. Table 3.6 highlights this idea.

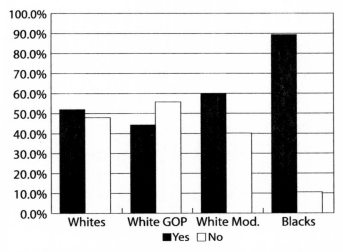

Figure 3.3. Bar chart of racial and ideological breakdown of responses to the question, "Do you believe that African Americans in Jacksonville experience racial discrimination in their daily lives?" Survey of Jacksonville Voters, 2004–2005, Public Opinion Research Laboratory at the University of North Florida, *N* = 803.

Most white Southerners do not welcome an active presence by government in addressing race relations. Black and Black (1987, 120) write about the "conservative advantage in public opinion" in the region. An important part of this conservative advantage is opinion about the role of government. White Southerners have long valued the idea of individual responsibility. Attitudes toward the national government have fluctuated. These fluctuations have ranged from hatred of the federal government after the Civil War to acceptance of assistance from New Deal programs to resentment of both taxes and spending brought on by the Great Society of the 1960s. This experience strongly contrasts with that of African Americans. Although it took 90 years from the end of the Civil War for results to manifest, the U.S. federal government, especially the courts, was the only government entity in the nation to assist African Americans in the early years of the civil rights struggle. Moreover, the Great Society programs of the 1960s directly assisted millions of black Southerners. While white Southerners tend to distrust government involvement in racial issues, black Southerners welcome such involvement as a necessary corrective to decades of discrimination.

Not only does disagreement exist over what government should do about race relations, strong differences are evident about which level of govern-

Table 3.7. Which Level of Government Would You Choose to Handle Important Political Issues that Matter to You?

	All Whites[a]	White Republicans[b]	White Moderates[c]	Blacks[d]
Federal government	31.9%	29.7%	29.5%	49.6%
State government	63.3%	65.6%	67.8%	47.7%
Local government	4.8%	4.8%	2.7%	2.8%

Source: Survey of Jacksonville Voters, 2004–2005. Public Opinion Research Laboratory, University of North Florida.
Notes: [a] $N = 570$
[b] $N = 355$
[c] $N = 215$
[d] $N = 331$

Table 3.8. Many Whites in Jacksonville Support the Republican Party, while Most Blacks in Jacksonville Support the Democratic Party. Does this Political Difference Harm Race Relations?

	All Whites[a]	White Republicans[b]	White Moderates[c]	Blacks[d]
Yes	30.0%	29.9%	29.6%	47.8%
No	70.0%	70.1%	70.4%	52.2%

Source: Survey of Jacksonville Voters, 2004–2005. Public Opinion Research Laboratory, University of North Florida.
Note: All Whites vs. all Blacks significant at $P \leq .05$ chi^2 statistic.
[a] $N = 581$
[b] $N = 365$
[c] $N = 223$
[d] $N = 343$

ment should address major issues. Table 3.7 shows that whites uniformly would rather have state government, rather than national government, handle important issues. In contrast with most whites, African Americans are more favorably inclined toward the national government. This difference of opinion may have its roots in white attitudes toward government in the post-civil rights South. The difference may also be greater if the question is posed when a Democrat holds the White House. In contrast to attitudes about the New Deal, many Southern whites see the Great Society programs as having primarily aided blacks. Also, because of economic growth in the

Table 3.9. Do You Believe that under Republican Leadership, Race Relations in Jackson-ville Will Improve, Get Worse, or Remain the Same?

	All Whites[a]	White Republicans[b]	White Moderates[c]	Blacks[d]
Improve	34.7%	46.4%	28.2%	18.9%
Get worse	8.9%	1.8%	9.3%	26.4%
Remain the same	56.5%	51.9%	62.6%	54.7%

Source: Survey of Jacksonville Voters, 2004-2005. Public Opinion Research Laboratory, University of North Florida.
Note: Whites vs. Blacks significant at $P \leq .05$ chi^2 statistic.
[a] $N = 601$
[b] $N = 375$
[c] $N = 231$
[d] $N = 357$

region in the 1950s and 1960s, many Southern whites began for the first time to pay substantial taxes during this period. Many of these white tax-payers do not perceive these programs as being beneficial to themselves, then or now. The combination of paying more money to government and not receiving perceived benefits in return heavily impacts white opinion regarding affirmative action and the role of the federal government (Black and Black 1987).

The current shift to the Republican Party in the region does not translate into much hope for African Americans. Table 3.8 shows that blacks and whites view the change in political party leadership quite differently.

African Americans are more pessimistic than are whites about the change in party leadership in the city. Almost half of African Americans surveyed said they believe that this difference will harm race relations while less than a third of whites view it the same way. As shown in Table 3.9, almost half of white Republicans believe that race relations in the city will actually improve under Republican leadership. Yet only 19% of African Americans believe this improvement will occur. Again, this question highlights the serious dif-ferences in perception between white Republicans and black Democrats. Given the chasm between each group's underlying beliefs, Republican op-timism about Republican leadership seems to be completely unfounded. White moderates do not share the optimism of white Republicans.

In sum, adding political partisanship to the South's pre-existing racial division presents a stark dilemma. White Republicans and black Democrats disagree on the presence of current discrimination; they disagree on the need for active government involvement to address discrimination; they disagree on which level of government should handle important issues, and they disagree (not surprisingly) on how effective Republican leadership will be in addressing race relations. Thus, 40 years after the civil rights movement, a wide separation exists between whites and African Americans on basic issues regarding race relations.

The added barrier of partisanship has made racial differences even more difficult to address. This is an important finding. V. O. Key believed that a major reason the South struggled with its political leadership in the 1940s was lack of party competition. This competitive void allowed segregation to dominate Southern politics and prevented economic and political progress. Today the South clearly has two competitive major parties, but this two-party system with its racial separation may not allow the political reform that Key envisioned. In fact, this two-party system may exacerbate racial differences.

If the Republican and Democratic parties in the South are going to remain racially separated, then white moderates, most of whom are Republican, will have to assume a much larger role in bridging both partisan and racial divisions. Without this leadership, partisan politics will increasingly polarize blacks and whites, as the following examples illustrate.

Florida Presidential Election of 2000 and Jacksonville

This separation can be highlighted by two recent elections in Jacksonville that left many local African Americans feeling politically isolated. In the controversial 2000 presidential election, George W. Bush clearly garnered more votes for president than did Al Gore in the city of Jacksonville. A total of 291,626 ballots were cast, and Bush received 152,460 (58%) compared to Gore's 108,039 (41%). There were 4,967 undervotes (when the vote counting machine does not detect a preference for any presidential candidate) and 21,942 overvotes (the machine detects a preference for more than one candidate).[2] This meant more than 9% of those who participated in the election did not have their vote tabulated for president. While such a figure would be disturbing in any democratically held election, a 9% vote loss would typically have minimal impact on an election's results, provided that the uncounted votes were randomly distributed. This was not the case in Jacksonville in 2000. Proportionally many more questionable ballots, especially

Figure 3.4. Duval County Supervisor of Elections John Stafford, *center*, talks with black elected officials about disqualified ballots in November 2000. (Photo reproduced by permission of the *Florida Times-Union*.)

Figure 3.5. Protestors outside the Supervisor of Elections Office in Duval County, Florida, in November 2000. (Photo reproduced by permission of the *Florida Times-Union*.)

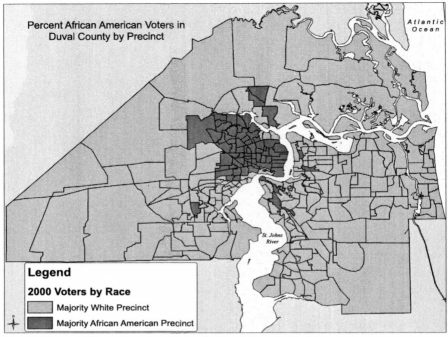

Map 3. Percent African American Voters in Duval County, Florida.

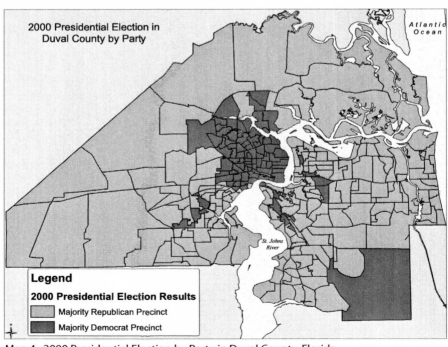

Map 4. 2000 Presidential Election by Party in Duval County, Florida.

the overvotes, came from the city's inner-core, which has the highest concentration of African American residents and Democratic voters. Given the closeness of the Florida election, these votes could have changed the outcome in the state and the nation. The number of ballots that were partially discarded was three times that of typical city elections. Because of a change in Florida law instituted prior to the 2000 election, the ballot featured 10 presidential candidates, with additional room for write-in candidates. The ballot for president covered two pages. Many of the overvotes were caused by voters punching a choice on every page. The ballot was longer than usual and confused some voters. Both Democratic Party leaders and civil rights leaders viewed the 2000 ballot and the overall voting process as examples of black voter disenfranchisement. Democratic leaders blamed the supervisor of elections office, which was headed by a Republican. The local chair of the Democratic Party said, "We have been, to put it bluntly, screwed" (DeCamp 2000, A2). The Republican supervisor of elections countered that the voters who made the mistakes were responsible: "We had a good ballot, very easy to understand. The voter needs to take responsibility" (DeCamp 2000).

Protestors highlighted the racial element of the controversy. One black protestor claimed that a local Republican told him, "If you do not like the system, go back to where you came from" (DeCamp 2000). The racial tensions became magnified as the recount controversy continued. Many blacks in the community believed that George W. Bush would never have been elected president if the rejected ballots had been tabulated. A Jacksonville University survey conducted after the election showed that local African Americans had little confidence in the electoral system. White Republicans rejected these claims as ridiculous. Either way, the 2000 presidential election served to increase racial tensions in the community. A local task force highlighted problems with the election process in Jacksonville, but the end result left many African Americans wary of the political process. Maps 3 and 4 highlight how race and party were heavily related in the controversial election of 2000.

Mayoral Election 2003

The second event that highlighted and intensified racial tensions in Jacksonville was the mayoral election in 2003. The general election featured Sheriff Nat Glover, an African American Democrat, versus John Peyton, a white

Republican businessman. Eight years earlier, Glover had won a considerable upset to be elected sheriff in 1995. After two terms as sheriff, he sought to become the first black mayor in the history of Jacksonville since Reconstruction. In contrast, Peyton was a political newcomer but he had the advantage of being an executive in his family's successful petroleum and real estate company. Peyton had access to many corporate leaders and he raised a record $2.5 million. He was the beneficiary of recent Republican voting trends in the area. Glover was attempting to put back together the biracial coalition that had elected him to the office of sheriff. Yet, due to the scars of the 2000 presidential election, racial and partisan voting patterns endured.

The mayoral campaign was competitive and tough throughout. However, during its last two weeks, the contest focused on race. Ten days prior to the election, racial graffiti appeared on Glover's campaign headquarters. Sprayed in black paint on his headquarters was the saying, "No Nigger Mayor" (DeCamp 2003). While both campaigns disavowed the graffiti, the racist sentiment highlighted racial divisions. Republicans floated the theory that Democrats had posted the graffiti as a set-up. Black leaders insisted that the incident was another example of blatant discrimination. A couple of days after the graffiti incident, the Glover campaign ran a commercial saying that his opponent, John Peyton, would be bad for African Americans in Jacksonville. The Peyton campaign countered that Glover's campaign was releasing "racial poison" into the political atmosphere (DeCamp 2003, A2). This kind of racially heated politics garnered national attention from the Associated Press and CNN. The outcome of the race revealed the racial divisions that had first become apparent in Jacksonville in 2000. Most of the inner core of the city supported Glover (D) with 42% of the vote; the rest of the city supported Peyton (R) with 58% of the vote (See map 5).

The failure to elect a well-liked African American sheriff as mayor highlights the political limitations that African American Democrats encounter in the region. White Republicans, led by their strength in the suburban and rural areas of the county, now dominate politics in the city.

Conclusion

The change in the South's political structure is important because it has combined racial separation with partisan division. Citizens' attitudes and recent events show the stark political and social divide between white Republicans and African American Democrats in Jacksonville. Yet, even with

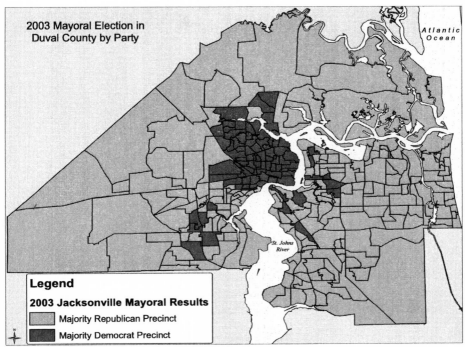

2003 Mayoral Election in
Duval County by Party

*Atlantic
Ocean*

*St. Johns
River*

Legend

2003 Jacksonville Mayoral Results

Majority Republican Precinct

Majority Democrat Precinct

Map 5. 2003 Mayoral Election by Party in Duval County, Florida.

doubts among whites about government's role in dealing with race relations
and doubts among African Americans about Republican leaders, both black
and white citizens view political leadership as important to race relations.

Extraordinary leadership would be required to seriously address race relations in a political context. The paradox of current Southern politics is that
political leadership is necessary to address racial division, but the current
political situation makes this type of leadership almost impossible. With
electoral political institutions that separate white Republicans and African
American Democrats, white leaders have little incentive to address racial issues on a fundamental level. In addition, black leaders who represent mostly
black citizens tend to ignore efforts to engage white citizens in addressing
racial and social concerns. For the most part, current African American
leaders have not adopted the political strategy of the civil rights movement
of the 1960s, which sought to engage white Southerners directly. In fact, cooperation with white Republicans is seen as a sellout. When African Ameri-

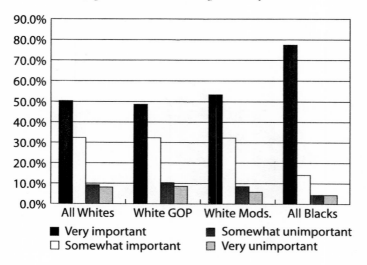

Figure 3.6. Bar chart of racial and ideological breakdown of responses to the question, "How important are elected political officials in helping to improve race relations?" Survey of Jacksonville Voters, 2004–2005, Public Opinion Research Laboratory at the University of North Florida, *N* = 948.

can Democrats run against each other for political office, these campaigns usually devolve into bitter fights over which candidate has worked the closest with Republicans (Rushing, 2006). African American organizations and columnists have criticized black elected officials in the city for their lack of leadership on important issues. Columnist Tonya Weathersbee called for a "rebirth of black leadership in the city and nation" (Weathersbee 2006).

The partisan aspect of this separation is also critical. White Republicans generally believe that government should be extremely limited in addressing social and economic inequalities. This conservative philosophy focuses on individual responsibility and family structure and downplays the historical impacts of slavery and segregation.

Many African American Democrats view social and economic inequalities through a completely different lens. Present and historical discrimination are central facts in the lives of African American Southerners. This view holds that government involvement is needed to address disparities that were caused by current and past discrimination. Yet, while black leaders look to government for leadership, many have been unwilling or unable to address many self-inflicted problems in the black community.

What are the impacts of such a stark divide between black and white perceptions of race? In Jacksonville, this division does not mean that blacks and whites avoid interacting in the political arena. African American and white city council members often work together on common issues involving the community. Black leadership is especially important in several independent agencies that operate under city government. African Americans and whites frequently cut deals in city politics. The nonprofit sector provides many programs that attempt to confront the challenges of the urban poor in the city. Despite these efforts, there remains a strong undercurrent of racial division in the community. This racial division may one day translate into social unrest in the form of protests or even violent confrontations.

Much depends on whether young African Americans join the political process. The data in this study do not examine nonvoters and as a result leave out many young citizens. The negative social indicators cited above disproportionately reflect the living conditions of young blacks in the community. Confrontations between young black males and the sheriff's office remain a source of racial division in the city. In 2006, a rise in the murder rate became a community crisis when two black girls under age 10 were shot in separate incidents in their homes. Young black men were arrested for these murders. After the 70th murder in the space of a year, the mayor and the sheriff joined with faith and business leaders to formalize a strategy. Police patrols were increased, and a day of faith was used to rally the community. Yet this issue also highlighted racial divisions in the community. The Republican sheriff initially had refused to commit more police officers to African American neighborhoods while the murder rate was accelerating (Schoettler 2006).

Not only young black teenagers are being impacted by racial tensions in Jacksonville. During 2006, the Jacksonville Fire Department was under investigation for a racial incident involving hanging nooses left for black firefighters near their lockers. White firefighters also recently sued the department for reverse discrimination. In a study on racial issues commissioned by the mayor, the local Human Rights Commission found that a "culture of discrimination" exists in the department. The commission recommended that the fire chief be removed. The mayor refused to comply, and tensions increased between the black community and the mayor. The local NAACP denounced the mayor. Investigations into the noose incident were inconclusive, with both a black and a white firefighter failing lie detector tests (Murphy 2006). This very public argument between successful firefighter professionals of different races highlights the depth of racial differences in the community (Murphy, 2006).

This is a difficult situation for any city to endure. Can white Republican leadership move beyond their slogans of small government and put together a coherent strategy to address racial disparities? Can African American Democrats engage white Republicans in meaningful and constructive ways? Answers to these questions may determine the future of the city and the region as a whole. The current gulf in attitudes between white Republicans and African American Democrats offers both a stark warning and a historical opportunity.

Finally, the basic premise of Southern race relations will be altered dramatically over the next decades. Hispanic immigrants from Puerto Rico, Mexico, and other Latin American nations are moving to the South in record numbers. While Texas and Florida have long had established Hispanic communities, Latino immigrants are spreading out across other parts of the South. According to the Pew Research Center, many of these new Hispanic residents are young males who come to the region for economic opportunity. They fill jobs primarily in the service, construction, and agriculture industries (Pew Hispanic Center 2005).

The political impacts of the Hispanic migration are uncertain. Many new immigrants are not citizens and thus do not vote. Other Hispanics who become citizens do not vote in proportion to their population, usually due to language barriers. (An exception is the Cuban immigrant community of Miami, who trend Republican). In Jacksonville, Latino voters make up only about 4% of voters. Yet the Latino population in the city is much greater than this voting percentage would indicate.

The key for Hispanic political involvement is mobility. Will most new Hispanic immigrants settle in one place and become part of the voting population? Or will these new Hispanic Southerners continually move on to the next job? These questions may not be answered for a generation. If the new Hispanic Southerners do become politically active, the political consequences are uncertain. This new migration may produce anti-immigration sentiment in both parties. African Americans and Hispanics could come together in the Democratic Party or they could be separated by ethnic and economic tensions. Will the Republican Party be able to assimilate new Hispanics in addition to the Florida Cuban residents who vote Republican? Former Florida governor Jeb Bush made this assimilation a major political priority and engaged in effective outreach to many Hispanic groups in the state. Because they claim different places of origin, Hispanics do not vote as a block. If either party can integrate more Hispanic voters into its voting coalition without losing its respective base, a new political system will be born in the region.

Southern Religion Meets Modern Politics

"I'm not here today on behalf of any other candidate than the Lord Jesus Christ" (Brumley 2004a, B1). These words were spoken by Ralph Reed, the former director of Pat Robertson's Christian Coalition, from the pulpit of Jacksonville's First Baptist Church on the last Sunday before the 2004 presidential election. Reed appeared on behalf of George W. Bush's 2004 presidential campaign and spoke to thousands of churchgoers. He did not directly ask for their vote from the pulpit, but his presence sent a clear signal to followers to support the incumbent.

To counter this religious appeal, vice-presidential candidate John Edwards appeared at an African American church in Jacksonville on the same day and urged black voters to support the Democrats and John Kerry (Brumley 2004a).

These examples show the depth of the connection between religion and politics in the South. This connection is so potent in some Southern regions that it can dominate politics, taking even some Southerners by surprise. "I've been in church all my life and I've never seen anything like this." This quote comes from a churchgoing Baptist woman in western North Carolina who was commenting on the expulsion of nine members from her church because they did not support George W. Bush in the 2004 election. Their pastor, Rev. Chan Chandler, told his congregation that if anyone planned to vote for John Kerry, "they should get up and leave" (Austin 2005, A1).

Many political observers have examined the nexus of religion and politics in the South (Dionne and Drogosz 2002; Fournier 2004). Surprisingly, this important topic has received little attention until recently from scholars of Southern politics. The dean of Southern political analysis, V. O. Key, hardly mentions the topic in his works. Earl Black and Merle Black write about conservative ideology and values, but they do not focus on religion. Green et al. (2003) are notable exceptions because they examine the importance of denomination and religious commitment in voting patterns. Wilcox (1994) also has chronicled the rise of the Religious Right and highlights the South in this examination. Both anecdotal and survey research show the important connection between politics and religion in the South. This chapter will examine this connection in the context of the South's new political system. If religion and attitudes about morality matter to politics in the region, what impact does this nexus have on the future of Southern politics and its leaders?

Part of scholars' reluctance to examine the nexus between religious beliefs and politics is due to the difficulty of defining words such as "values" and "beliefs." While philosophers and religious scholars may be skilled in navigating these waters, political analysts often are not. Morality can mean many things to different people. Morality implies setting specific standards of conduct by which to live. Some of these standards, such as prohibitions against murder or the stealing of someone's property, are universally accepted. Other standards are not so clear-cut. For instance, should society/government regulate personal sexual behavior? Should moral values force government to address the serious poverty that occurs in the United States and around the world? Should government regulate the content of movies, music and other forms of entertainment when they contain violence and sex?

Answers to questions like these enter the political process in the United States through political campaigns, legislation, and the courts. Yet, political responses to these issues may be unsatisfying because the U.S. political process depends on compromise. Those who seek to resolve moral dilemmas through the political process may strongly believe that no compromise is possible on their core beliefs. Conflict between moral certainty and political reality is inevitable. Yet this conflict has not stopped moral and religious factors from becoming central to American politics.

Belief in certain moral standards may have a powerful impact on political beliefs. In a comprehensive examination of moral and cultural attitudes and their impact on politics, Leege et al. (2002, 5) state that citizens "have a sense of a legitimate social order and they expect other citizens and their government to further that design." These ideas of moral order do not vary from election to election; they are inherent. Accordingly, if political consultants can tap into these ideas, they can access feelings and ideas that may excite and activate voters. For example, the chances that gay marriage will become legal in any Southern state in the near future are negligible. However, this low probability has not stopped political consultants from using this issue in Southern campaigns. Matthew Dowd, President Bush's pollster for the 2004 election, said that elections "are always about values," not issues (Thomas 2006).

Concerns over values animate many local, state, and presidential campaigns in the South. For instance, in the 2004 Florida U.S. Senate campaign, candidate Mel Martinez attacked fellow Republican Bill McCollum as the "darling of homosexual extremists" because McCollum once supported a hate crimes bill that included protection of homosexuals (Debose 2004, A4). The charge was surprising because McCollum had a solid conservative record, including having served as a House manager of the Clinton impeachment trial in 1998 and 1999. Martinez won the tough primary battle and went on to win a close general election. As the Republican primary battle between Martinez and McCollum shows, controversy over moral beliefs can be a deciding factor in Southern political races.

Yet in terms of political impact, these beliefs do not occur in a vacuum. For moral issues to become important in the political process, it is not enough for voters to hold certain moral beliefs. They must act on these beliefs. They must be mobilized. Organized religion offers a means to achieve this mobilization. Wald et al. (1988) found that when a voter joins a church and ascribes to that church's beliefs, these religious beliefs have a powerful impact on the individual's political beliefs. Churches and other religious centers make up the largest number of voluntary associations in the nation. They are the places where people with similar beliefs come together on a weekly basis. The most skilled political operative in the world cannot match this type of mobilization and organization. Targeting church groups and religious associations enables candidates and consultants to skip the step of trying to mobilize and organize individuals. Instead, they can concentrate on mobilizing groups of thousands of voters and potential voters. To preserve their tax-exempt status, religious organizations cannot outwardly endorse political candidates, but this regulation has become almost meaningless. Churches and religious leaders in the South clearly make their political preferences known by printing voter guides, adding political inserts to church bulletins, sponsoring personal appearances with candidates, and making indirect appeals to congregations.

These religious affiliations offer the candidate and the party that will adopt his or her views the opportunity to influence millions of voters. Historically, most of the politically active churches in the South were various denominations of Protestants. While Protestants still dominate the religious landscape of the South, today the region is much more complex. Catholics have become targets for the Republican Party. Also, mainline Protestant churches have seen their congregations shrink as evangelical Protestant churches have expanded dramatically.

As chapter 3 has shown, examining the racial history of the region further highlights the need for greater examination of the connection of religion and politics in Southern politics. Simply put, the civil rights movement, which fundamentally altered Southern politics, would not have occurred without African American churches and religious leadership.

The 1955 Montgomery bus boycott began with meetings in the city's churches. Rev. Martin Luther King Jr. led the Southern Christian Leadership Conference in nonviolent confrontation of segregation. King's eloquent letter from a Birmingham jail in 1963 made explicit references to his religious beliefs. When Birmingham ministers questioned why King was leading protests, he responded: "one has a moral responsibility to disobey unjust laws, I would agree with St. Augustine that 'an unjust law is no law at all.'" (King 1963). The murder of four black girls in a Birmingham church bombing galvanized opposition to segregation and shocked the conscience of most white Southerners. Black ministers led the final triumphant march from Selma to Montgomery with participation by white ministers and priests.

Black churches offered the civil rights movement precious assets for political mobilization. For a segment of the population with little economic clout, black churches offered substantial financial and in-kind assets. The group structure of churches offered ready-made units of organization for political participation. Most importantly, black churches offered leadership. Almost all of the important leaders of the civil rights movement were religious leaders as well. From the beginning, this tradition of combining religion and politics in the black community continues today. Many African Americans expect their ministers and churches to be politically active.

In contrast with black churchgoers, white Protestants in the South have experienced substantially different intersections between religion and politics. While the impact of religion on Southern life has always been substantial (Hill 1966), the connection between religion and politics in the region was inconsistent until the last 25 years. In the solid Democratic South that dominated Southern politics through the 1950s, there was little need for churches to be involved in politics. Most Southerners were conservative Democrats who voted Democratic under almost any circumstance. (A notable exception was 1928 when Al Smith, a Catholic from New York, ran for president on the Democratic ticket.) Moreover, two major events in the early twentieth century, Prohibition and the Scopes Monkey Trial, left many Southern church leaders wary of political involvement. Prohibition was a victory for leaders who wanted a more temperate society without alcohol. Yet, the victory was short lived. Citizens either outwardly flouted Prohibition laws or complained vigorously about them. In the South, moonshine production became an art unto itself. Prior to the repeal of the Eighteenth Amendment, much of the criticism about it was directed at the involvement of church leaders.

The so-called Scopes Monkey Trial of 1925, during which fundamentalists (those who believe in the literal interpretation of the Bible) put a teacher in Tennessee on trial for teaching evolution, was a turning point. Fundamentalists won the court case but lost the public relations battle (Reichley 2002). The Northern press portrayed Southern fundamentalists as zealots who declared war on science. Today, a similar argument is being fought over allowing intelligent design into the classroom. In Georgia, a school board went to federal court to protect their policy of integrating intelligent design into the curricula of biology classes (Hart 2004).

Just as they had been targeted for advocating Prohibition, so were white church leaders criticized for their role in bringing *Tennessee v. John Scopes* to trial. Again, this criticism left many citizens wary of politics and policy issues. Since most Southerners supported one political party anyway, many white churches withdrew from outward political activity. For decades, white Protestant conservatives believed that "churches should devote themselves to individual salvation and had no business mixing religion with politics" (Reichley 2002, 239).

This attitude changed dramatically in the 1970s and 1980s. The cultural and political revolutions of the 1960s created a strong backlash among white evangelical Christians. Evangelicals believe in salvation through Jesus Christ by having a "born-again" experience, following the literal word of the Bible, and taking on responsibility to aggressively spread the word of God (Wilcox 1994).[1] The images of casual sex, drug use, and flouting of authority being broadcast on television screens during the time provoked church leaders into action. The 1973 *Roe v. Wade* decision, which asserted a woman's constitutional right to abortion, further galvanized evangelical Protestants as well as Catholic leaders. Many white Protestant church leaders openly supported Democratic candidate Jimmy Carter in 1976 because Carter proudly proclaimed himself to be a born-again Christian. This support helped Carter retake most of the South in the 1976 presidential election, the last time a Democratic presidential candidate won most of the South. Yet, conservative Christians quickly became upset with Carter because he did not take more aggressive positions to oppose abortion during his term as president.

In the 1980 presidential election, Republican candidate Ronald Reagan made an overt effort to win over Southern white Christian conservatives. This election became a critical turning point that helped white Christian conservatives become the base of the Republican Party. At a meeting of evangelical preachers in the 1980 campaign, Reagan cleverly stated that while he was not asking for their endorsement, he admitted that "I endorse you and what you are doing" (Raines 1980, A8). At the same meeting, Reagan applauded when minister James Robison declared that government was "public enemy number 1. .". . I'm sick and tired of hearing about all of the radicals and the perverts and the liberals and the leftists and the Communists coming out the closet; it's time for God's people to come out of the closet" (Raines 1980, A8).

Accordingly, the Southern Baptist Convention became much more vocal about politics and more conservative in the 1980s and 1990s. The convention moved to purge established mainline leaders from leadership positions and to take a more active role in political affairs. Evangelical minister and televangelist Pat Robertson ran for president in 1988 and did well in the Iowa caucuses, although he did not secure the Republican nomination. Political activity among white evangelicals continued in the 1990s. Many observers have credited the mobilization of white evangelical conservatives with the 1994 Republican takeover of Congress (Wilcox 1994).

Recent national Republican leadership displays the strong connection between religion and politics. Then-presidential candidate George W. Bush said in 2000 that his favorite political philosopher was Jesus Christ because he changed his heart (Firestone 2000, A18). This statement sent an explicit message to Christian conservatives that Bush was one of them. In 2005, during George Bush's second term, Republican Senate Majority leader Bill Frist appeared with many conservative Christian preachers on the TV show *Justice Sunday*. This program brought together Christian preachers who believed that judges were not upholding moral standards.

These white evangelical conservatives represent the heart of the connection between religion and politics for Republicans in the South. They are a driving force within the party. Yet, it is crucial to note that not only have Republicans done well with white evangelical voters in the South, they also have done very well with mainline Protestant denominations and white Catholic voters. Without the support of mainline white Protestants and white Catholics, the recent Republican success would not have been as extensive. In exit polls after the close 2000 presidential election, white Southern Protestants (evangelical and mainline) said they voted for Bush by a margin of 70% to 28% in the South, and white Catholics went for Bush by more than a 2–1 margin. Evangelicals may receive most of the media's attention, but mainline Protestants and white Catholics also have aided Republicans tremendously.

These examples highlight the trends apparent in the data presented in chapter 1. While national political observers may be loudly arguing about the separation of church and state, the debate has been settled in Southern politics. No one makes the serious argument that organized religion should become one with government, yet religious beliefs and organized religious activities are heavily intertwined with politics in the region. The question becomes, How does this connection impact the political order of the region? Furthermore, how does this connection help or hinder the future challenges that Southern society must confront with new Republican leadership?

Figure 4.1. Rev. Jerry Vines, then-pastor of First Baptist Church, in downtown Jacksonville. The church has more than 28,000 members. (Photo reproduced by permission of the *Florida Times-Union*.)

Religious Profile of Jacksonville, Florida

Religion and church-centered activities are critical elements of life in Jacksonville. Religious elements even pervade sports events, including national championship games held in the city. For example, during the 39th Super Bowl (the highest profile event a city can host) held in Jacksonville on February 6, 2005, Christian conservatives made their presence known. The event was described as the most religious Super Bowl ever. With media from all over the country converging on the city, local churches gathered their members and marched downtown to remind their followers not to enjoy too much revelry. This procession followed on the heels of the mayor's declaration, one week prior to the Super Bowl, that January 29 was "Super March for Jesus" day in the city (Fridell 2005, B1).

Other indicators of the centrality of religion in the community abound. Even with a large population of 800,000, the city did not allow liquor sales on Sunday until 1989. The First Baptist Church in downtown Jacksonville is the largest landowner in the core city area. Moreover, nearly 50% of voters attend church at least once a week. To understand the strong influence of organized religion and religious beliefs on politics in Jacksonville, two aspects of religious life must be examined: religious affiliations/traditions and religious commitment (Green et al. 2003).

Religious Affiliations

Jacksonville has more than 300 places of worship. Baptist churches are the most numerous, with more than 120 locations for Baptist services. The Baptist tradition also represents the racial separation of Jacksonville's churches. In 1838 the most prominent Baptist church in the city split along racial lines. The Bethel Baptist Church became the church for black slaves and black citizens. Prominent white members broke off and started the First Baptist Church in downtown Jacksonville. The racial division represented by these two churches mirrors that found in most parts of the South (Bartley 2000; Green et al. 2003).

To this day, Bethel remains Jacksonville's most prominent African American church, and the First Baptist Church is a religious, economic and political power in the city. Many Jacksonville political leaders are associated with First Baptist Church, which has more than 28,000 members. Yet, the Baptist tradition is only part of the religious makeup of the city. Table 4.1 shows a mixture of mainline Protestant denominations (Episcopal, Lutheran, Presbyterian, Methodist), along with Catholics, Jewish congregations, and several new evangelical groups that claim no denomination.

Table 4.1. Jacksonville Voters' Religious Denominations

	Whites[a]	Blacks[b]	All[c]
Southern Baptist	22.9%	51.0%	28.1%
Methodist	9.3%	4.7%	7.3%
Presbyterian	5.2%	1.3%	4.2%
Episcopalian	7.1%	2.6%	6.1%
Lutheran	3.7%	0.2%	2.8%
Catholic	19.9%	4.3%	16.6%
Jewish	2.0%	0.2%	1.6%
Other Protestant	8.3%	17.5%	11.5%
Other	11.1%	10.4	11.5%
No religion or atheist	10.6%	7.7%	10.3%

Source: Survey of Jacksonville Voters, 2004-2005. Public Opinion Research Laboratory, University of North Florida.
Notes:
[a] $N = 653$
[b] $N = 382$
[c] $N = 931$

African Americans have a wide variety of different denominations that are almost exclusively Protestant. Yet, in terms of political behavior, African Americans of almost all religious denominations still support the Democratic Party. More than 80% of African Americans in Jacksonville identify with the Democratic Party. This stark fact guides this examination in important ways. In terms of public opinion, African Americans are more unified than are white voters, as shown in chapter 3. Accordingly, it is necessary to examine variations among white voters and their connection to religion. It is for white voters that Republicans and Democrats truly compete. Many political consultants and observers have criticized the Democratic Party for losing white voters who are concerned about moral values (Bai 2005; Shaffrey 2005).

Baptists are clearly a cultural and political force in the city. With nearly 30,000 members and extensive real estate holdings, the First Baptist Church downtown is the cornerstone of this power. Its former pastor, Jerry Vines, was part of a successful campaign in the Southern Baptist Convention to make that national organization more conservative. The last Sunday before the 2000 presidential election, candidate George W. Bush came to Jacksonville to worship with Vines and other ministers. Presidential advisor Karl Rove contacted Reverend Vines in 2005 to assure him that Supreme Court nominee Harriet Miers had the right values and that Vines could be "com-

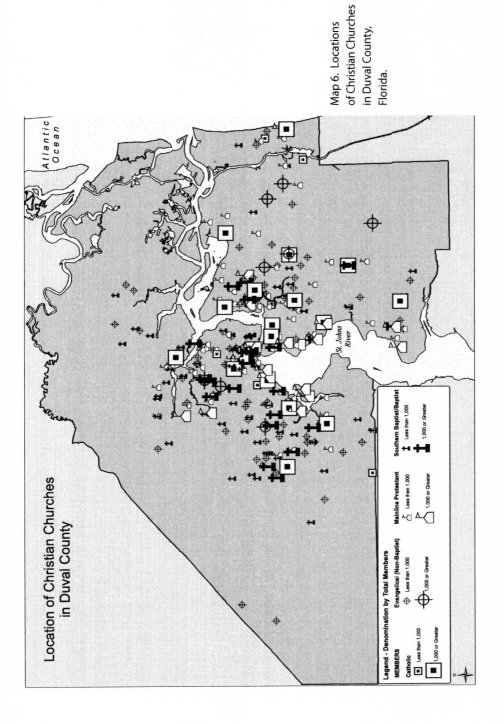

Map 6. Locations of Christian Churches in Duval County, Florida.

fortable" with her. (Brumley 2005, A1). Similarly, most political candidates in Jacksonville make a point of visiting the church at least once during campaign season.

While the importance of megachurches like First Baptist has received analytical notice in recent years (Kelly and Conlon 2005), these large churches do not have a monopoly on political clout. The influence of organized religion in politics in the South is not confined to these super churches; rather, the pervasive power of combining organized religion and politics lies in the number of different churches that are ripe to be involved in the political process. As shown in map 6, hundreds of churches, both large and small, cover the city. Along the St. Johns River, in the older part of the city, many mainline Protestant churches still remain. Yet, in the growing part of the city to the south and the west, Baptist and new nondenominational evangelical churches dominate. The diversity and broad distribution of churches in Jacksonville is precisely why the Republican National Committee took the unprecedented step in 2004 of directly requesting church directories from Protestant and Catholic churches (Zoll 2004).

Thus, the large First Baptist Church is not alone in its influence on politics. Political candidates cannot visit every house of worship, but they can take positions and give signals to voters that they share their religious beliefs. In contrast with Democrats, Republicans have been much stronger at speaking this language to white Christian conservatives, by focusing on issues such as abortion, gay marriage, and prayer at public events. In recent years, Democrats have rarely talked about public policy in religious or moral terms. This reticence is surprising, given that 40 years ago Martin Luther King Jr. led one of the most successful political movements in the region's history by placing social and economic justice as moral imperatives. Democrats have been unable to balance the party's differences between secular voters and religious voters.

Among white voters in Jacksonville, Catholics now represent almost one-fifth of voters. This finding would not have been possible 30 years ago in the city. The growth of the Catholic Church in the South has been steady and constant. This growth is concentrated in metropolitan areas, especially suburban areas (Grammich 2005). This growth has had important political impacts. Catholics now join with other conservative Christian groups to present a unified front on issues such as opposition to abortion and gay marriage. This alliance between Catholics and evangelical Protestants is significant due to the historically tense relationship between these two religious groups.

Table 4.2. White Respondents' Religious Denominations by Political Party Identification

	Dem.[a]	GOP[b]
Southern Baptist	14.2%	28.0%
Methodist	9.0%	8.2%
Presbyterian	7.5%	5.0%
Episcopalian	3.0%	8.2%
Lutheran	3.0%	3.5%
Catholic	21.6%	18.4%
Jewish	5.2%	1.2%
Other Protestant	8.2%	10.6%
Other	14.2%	10.4%
No religion or atheist	14.2%	6.5%

Source: Survey of Jacksonville Voters, 2004-2005. Public Opinion Research Laboratory, University of North Florida.
Notes:
a N = 134
b N = 403

The local Catholic bishop has taken strong official positions on matters such as gay marriage and the Terri Schiavo case. The latter concerned a brain-damaged woman with a feeding tube, whose husband fought for her right to die. The bishop stood with a group of protestors in front of the Jacksonville Federal Courthouse to demand that Terri Schiavo be kept alive (Pinkham, 2005). The bishop also has joined with the Florida Baptist Convention to support a constitutional initiative to ban gay marriage in Florida (Brumley 2004c).

This type of political activism on behalf of conservative social issues is an important change for the American Catholic Church. While opposition to the *Roe v. Wade* decision of 1973 has been a constant refrain from the Catholic bishops, the 1970s and 1980s saw other forms of social activism. In the 1980s, two important pastoral letters from American bishops warned the nation about the dangers of continuing the nuclear arms race and urged the United States to begin to redistribute its wealth to the poor. While American bishops have not altered their stances on these issues, the relative importance of these issues has changed. The emergence of increasingly conservative cardinals and bishops in the 1990s has established a hierarchy of issues (Reichley 2002). This hierarchy places abortion and gay marriage above other public policy issues. This shift in emphasis obviously aids the platform of the Republican Party. This advantage has regional foundations.

While party loyalties among Catholics are nearly divided nationally, white Southern Catholics voted for Republican presidential candidates by a 2–1 margin in 2000 and 2004, according to exit polls. This shift in emphasis has allowed many conservative Catholics when voting to basically ignore the other concerns coming from Rome about the excesses of capitalism and issues addressing the poor.

The emphasis on conservative social issues may influence Hispanic Catholics to look at the Republican Party as well. In many parts of the South, an increasing number of Hispanics is adding to the ranks of Catholics. The political impact of Hispanic Catholics is uncertain because Hispanic Catholics are so varied. In Florida, Cuban Hispanics support Republicans for the party's strong anti-Castro stance. Yet, newly arrived Mexican immigrants may be persuaded by economic arguments of Democratic candidates. Other Latinos from Central and South America may have their own issues and trends. However, if Republicans take a strong anti-immigration stance, Hispanic Catholics may go Democratic.

As previously mentioned, conservative Christian Protestant groups need white Catholics for political support. While these Protestants are the core of the Republican Party in the South, they do not have the numbers to win elections or change policies on their own in larger metropolitan areas. They need a majority of white Catholics and mainline Protestants to join them under the Republican banner. Realistically, Democrats will not win back many white evangelical Christians in the near future; the real dilemma for Democrats is understanding how they have lost so many white mainline Protestants and Catholics. Not surprisingly, the first Republican mayor of Jacksonville since Reconstruction, elected in 1995, was Catholic.

Other religious denominations are part of the religious makeup of the city. Five Jewish synagogues have long been present in Jacksonville. Many Jewish adults are an important part of the professional makeup of the community. The city also has one of the largest Christian Palestinian expatriate populations in the United States. Several mosques are also present, and Muslims have built a Northeast Florida Islamic Center. The numbers of these denominations are small in comparison to those of Catholic and Protestant places of worship, but they are growing.

Activism and Attendance

Like voters in other parts of the South, Jacksonville voters are attached and committed to religious affiliations. An important measure of religious commitment is church/worship attendance. High commitment shows a greater attachment to a religious tradition (Green et al. 2003). As noted, no one religious denomination dominates Southern politics. Moreover, Southern voters of all political parties tend to have a religious denomination and believe in God. The defining religious factors that have helped to identify Republican voters in recent years are church attendance and belief in religious tradition, not merely having a religious affiliation. The *Pew Forum on Religion and Public Life* examined 2004 exit polls and concluded:

> "By far the most powerful reality at the intersection of religion and politics is this: Americans who regularly attend worship services and hold traditional religious beliefs increasingly vote Republican, while those who are less connected to religious institutions. . . . tend to vote Democratic" (Pew Forum 2005).

Accordingly, those who attend church regularly were an important target group for the Bush campaigns in 2000 and 2004. Church attendance and activism are political indicators that unite white Republicans of different denominations. The Jacksonville survey shows that most voters in the city are highly committed, with more than 68% of voters attending church at least twice a month and 50% attending at least once a week.

The centrality of religion in Jacksonville politics is evident. To understand the impact of religious and moral concerns on the political attitudes of Jacksonville citizens under the new Republican leadership, three questions need to be addressed:

1. How concerned are voters about moral/religious issues?
2. If they are concerned, then what role should religion and places of worship have in addressing these concerns politically?
3. If these concerns are to be addressed politically, who should address them and how?

To gain a clearer picture of the impact of religion and morality on the politics in the region, different political groups must be compared. As previously stated, the fact that over 80% of African Americans consistently support the Democratic Party and that church membership is heavily segregated point the researcher to separate whites and African Americans when making comparisons. The oversample of African Americans makes these comparisons possible. The emergence of the Republican Party in Southern politics directs the researcher to compare these attitudes by political party. The Pew Forum describes the importance of religion and church attendance as a "faith-based partisan divide," with Republicans doing very well with churchgoers (Pew Forum on Religion and Public Life 2005). This partisan divide is examined below.

Concern about Moral and Religious Issues

Are Jacksonville voters concerned about moral and religious issues? The answer appears to be an overwhelming yes. As shown in table 4.3, all of the city's demographic groups are very or somewhat concerned with moral values in the United States. The power of moral values as a political issue is demonstrated here. Concerns about morality are not confined to one party or race. However the concept is defined, morality has saliency among voters. Yet, it is unclear whether voters agree on what constitutes morality. Table 4.4 and figure 4.2 display attitudes about two current issues that are important to religious voters.

The data show that whites and African Americans show similar attitudinal patterns on the issues of abortion and gay marriage. Moreover, white churchgoing Republican voters also have much more in common with African Americans on religion and morality than do African Americans and white Democrats. Thus, the two critical support groups for both parties (African Americans for Democrats and white churchgoers for Republicans) tend to have some level of agreement on major cultural issues. This similarity in views can be seen on the national level as well (Busmiller and Kornblut 2005).

Table 4.3. How Concerned Are You that the Moral Values of the United States Are Declining?

	All Whites[a]	White GOP[b]	White Churchgoing GOP[c]	White Dem.[d]	All Blacks[e]
Very concerned	69.8%	77.8%	84.2%	54.1%	77.0%
Somewhat concerned	20.6%	15.4%	10.7%	30.6%	15.2%
Somewhat unconcerned	6.2%	4.3%	1.8%	9.8%	4.1%
Very unconcerned	3.4%	2.6%	3.3%	5.5%	3.6%

Source: Survey of Jacksonville Voters, 2004-2005. Public Opinion Research Laboratory, University of North Florida.
Note: Blacks vs. Whites significant at $P \leq .05$ chi^2 statistic.
[a] $N = 644$
[b] $N = 409$
[c] $N = 252$
[d] $N = 130$
[e] $N = 377$

Table 4.4. Are You More Pro-life or Pro-choice?

	All Whites[a]	White GOP[b]	White Churchgoing GOP[c]	White Dem[d]	All Blacks[e]
Pro-life	53.5%	68.6%	78.5%	21.9%	55.5%
Pro-choice	46.5%	31.4%	21.5%	78.1%	44.5%

Source: Survey of Jacksonville Voters, 2004-2005. Public Opinion Research Laboratory, University of North Florida.
Notes:
[a] $N = 629$
[b] $N = 392$
[c] $N = 245$
[d] $N = 129$
[e] $N = 357$

These data also help explain why issues such as abortion and gay rights surface in Southern political campaigns. These topics motivate churchgoing conservatives and isolate white Democrats. They present a frame through which voters can view candidates as either religious or not. The policy outcomes of these issues are less important than their symbolic value. Unless the Supreme Court overrules *Roe v. Wade*, most Southern states will continue to attempt to restrict abortions but not outlaw them. Moreover, gay

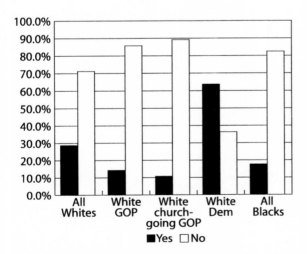

Figure 4.2. Bar chart of racial and church-attendance breakdown of responses to the question, "Do you support or oppose allowing same-sex couples the right to get married?" Survey of Jacksonville Voters, 2004–2005. Public Opinion Research Laboratory at the University of North Florida, $N = 948$.

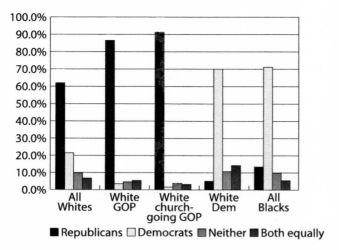

Figure 4.3. Bar chart of racial and church-attendance breakdown of responses to the question, "Which political party do you trust more on moral and cultural issues?" Survey of Jacksonville Voters, 2004–2005. Public Opinion Research Laboratory at the University of North Florida, $N = 948$.

marriages will not be legal in any of the Southern states in the foreseeable future. Thus, changes in public policy are less important to voters than the symbolic identity of these issues. It is a form of identity politics that may overcome other candidate positions and characteristics. If candidates do not share voters' "legitimate sense of order," it matters little what else the candidate or party can do. Republicans use the term *liberal* to describe political opponents who do not share these values. It is a symbolic word that easily might be translated, "someone who is not a religious Southerner."

If the true competition for voters in the South is among white voters, then these high-profile moral issues help to reveal clear distinctions between Democrats and Republicans. These issues also isolate white Democrats in their own party since African Americans are conservative on social issues.

Bringing Together Religious Beliefs and Political Action

Although voters may believe that moral and religious concerns are important, this belief does not automatically mean that voters want these concerns addressed politically. Do voters in Jacksonville and other places in the South want to integrate their moral concerns with political action? The data in table 4.5 provide guidance on this question. Again, among all demographic

Table 4.5. How Important Are Your Religious Values in Determining Your Political Beliefs?

	All Whites[a]	White GOP[b]	White Churchgoing GOP[c]	White Dem.[d]	All Blacks[e]
Very important	42.7%	51.0%	62.2%	25.5%	63.9%
Somewhat important	27.5%	27.7%	25.9%	29.0%	20.5%
Somewhat unimportant	13.4%	11.2%	6.1%	19.1%	6.5%
Very unimportant	16.5%	10.1%	5.8%	26.3%	9.2%

Source: Survey of Jacksonville Voters, 2004-2005. Public Opinion Research Laboratory, University of North Florida.
Note: All Whites vs. All Blacks significant at P ≤ .05 chi^2 statistic.
[a] $N = 592$
[b] $N = 383$
[c] $N = 251$
[d] $N = 117$
[e] $N = 353$

groups identified, religious values are important in determining political beliefs.

Not only do voters connect their own moral/religious beliefs with politics, they also expect political candidates and leaders to do the same. The data in table 4.6 highlight this expectation.

This is an interesting finding in light of the cynicism and distrust that many Americans have felt toward political leaders since Watergate in the 1970s. Faith in government and political leaders has dropped dramatically

Table 4.6. How Important Is It to You that Elected Officials Have Strong Moral Character?

	All Whites[a]	White GOP[b]	White Churchgoing GOP[c]	White Dem.[d]	All Blacks[e]
Very important	83.6%	91.1%	94.6%	71.4%	87.4%
Somewhat important	12.8%	7.2%	4.5%	19.7%	8.4%
Somewhat unimportant	1.7%	0.6%	0.0%	4.0%	3.0%
Very unimportant	1.9%	1.1%	0.9%	4.9%	1.1%

Source: Survey of Jacksonville Voters, 2004-2005. Public Opinion Research Laboratory, University of North Florida.
Notes:
[a] $N = 655$
[b] $N = 407$
[c] $N = 254$
[d] $N = 133$
[e] $N = 378$

Table 4.7. How Important Is It to You that the President of the United States Be a Religious Person?

	All Whites[a]	White GOP[b]	White Churchgoing GOP[c]	White Dem.[d]	All Blacks[e]
Very important	46.9%	59.1%	69.2%	26.4%	56.8%
Somewhat important	26.7%	26.4%	23.1%	27.3%	22.7%
Somewhat unimportant	11.7%	8.5%	5.9%	19.8%	9.6%
Very unimportant	14.6%	6.1%	1.8%	26.5%	10.8%

Source: Survey of Jacksonville Voters, 2004-2005. Public Opinion Research Laboratory, University of North Florida.

Notes:
[a] $N = 658$
[b] $N = 408$
[c] $N = 253$
[d] $N = 135$
[e] $N = 376$

since the 1960s. In 1998, a president was impeached by the House of Representatives because of a sexual affair he had with an intern. As of this writing, several Republican leaders, including former representative Tom Delay from Texas, are being investigated on corruption charges. The Mark Foley scandal, in which a congressman from Florida was caught pursuing young male congressional pages, dominated the news prior to the 2006 congressional elections. Even after decades of witnessing high-profile political scandals, voters still want their elected officials to exhibit high moral standards and religious faith. Above all, Southern voters expect their president to be religious. This desire is present among Jacksonville voters as well, as shown in table 4.7.

Again, the only group that lacks a majority of voters who believe the president and other candidates should be religious is white Democrats. Not surprisingly, churchgoing Republicans (nearly 70%) want their president to be religious. This expectation makes it inevitable that most candidates looking for votes in the South will talk about how important their religion is in their personal lives. Yet, their religious beliefs cannot be *all* they offer to voters. Candidates such as Roy Moore, the "Ten Commandments judge" from Alabama, and Randall Terry, the anti-abortion activist who ran for the Florida State Senate, both failed to be elected in 2006 because voters rejected their one-dimensional campaigns.

If many people in the South want their political leaders to show their

Table 4.8. Do You Agree or Disagree with the Following Statement? Religious Leaders Should Stay out of Politics and Public Affairs.

	All Whites[a]	White GOP[b]	White Churchgoing GOP[c]	White Dem.[d]	All Blacks[e]
Strongly agree	35.6%	29.1%	20.9%	41.6%	24.5%
Somewhat agree	15.8%	17.0%	14.5%	15.3%	14.2%
Somewhat disagree	21.6%	23.3%	26.0%	21.0%	17.9%
Strongly disagree	27.1%	30.5%	38.6%	22.1%	43.4%

Source: Survey of Jacksonville Voters, 2004-2005. Public Opinion Research Laboratory, University of North Florida.

Note: All Whites vs. All Blacks significant at $P \leq .05$ chi^2 statistic.

[a] $N = 643$
[b] $N = 409$
[c] $N = 247$
[d] $N = 130$
[e] $N = 375$

religious faith, is it also true that Southerners expect their religious leaders to be involved in politics? The answer appears to be yes. As noted earlier, African American churches have made it clear that their leaders will be politically involved. Similarly, white Protestant churches and Catholic churches have increased their outward political activity in recent decades. Scholars, Libertarians, and civil liberty groups have warned against religious leaders becoming directly involved in political affairs (Greely 2002). These critics are concerned that a democratic representative government may slowly devolve into a political theocracy. Yet, voters in Jacksonville and other parts of the South are ignoring these warnings. As shown in table 4.8, voters in most groups profiled look to their religious leaders for political involvement.

Again, white churchgoing Republicans and African Americans are in similar agreement on the involvement of religious leaders in politics. In contrast, white Democrats have the most reservations about mixing religious leadership and politics. Yet, many Jacksonville voters have little hesitation about looking to their religious leaders for political guidance. Among African Americans, black ministers are seen as an important voice in the community. When the current Republican mayor in Jacksonville won his first term with little African American support, he met with African American ministers on the day after the election. As mentioned above, prominent white Baptist ministers have been heavily involved in local and national politics. On the last Sunday prior to the 2004 election, former pastor Jerry

Table 4.9. Which Political Party Has More Leaders with Strong Moral Character?

	All Whites[a]	White GOP[b]	White Churchgoing GOP[c]	White Dem.[d]	All Blacks[e]
Democrats	13.1%	1.1%	1.3%	53.2%	54.0%
GOP	59.4%	81.1%	84.5%	6.2%	19.4%
Other	1.1%	0.9%	1.3%	0.0%	0.9%
About the same	14.0%	10.1%	7.8%	22.6%	16.3%
None	12.4%	6.9%	5.0%	18.1%	9.4%

Source: Survey of Jacksonville Voters, 2004-2005. Public Opinion Research Laboratory, University of North Florida.
Note: All Whites vs. All Blacks significant at P ≤ .05 chi^2 statistic.
[a] $N = 547$
[b] $N = 354$
[c] $N = 230$
[d] $N = 98$
[e] $N = 300$

Vines of the First Baptist Church in Jacksonville said that the election was not focused on "the economy stupid, it is the moral, ethical and spiritual issues that are paramount" (Brumley 2004, B1). He then asked everyone in the congregation to stand up if they were going to vote.

While it is clear that many Jacksonville voters agree that moral/religious values and politics are connected, there is less consensus on who should carry this message and what this message should be. White Republicans and African Americans generally agree on the need for morality in politics and the need for religious leaders in politics; they do not agree on the relative importance of various moral and cultural issues. An African American minister at an African Methodist church in Jacksonville said in an interview after the 2004 election that his definitions of moral values depended on race: "I believe my issues as a black man . . . are different from your issues as a white man, but no more important or less important or more moral or less moral" (Brumley 2004b, B1). African Americans tend to believe that economic justice issues are more important political priorities than are conservative social issues.

Blacks and whites also do not agree on which party should lead the effort to integrate morality and religion into politics. Clearly, morality and religiosity are in the eye of the beholder. In table 4.9, clear disagreement exists on which party has more leaders with strong moral character.

Table 4.10. Which Political Party Do You Trust More on National Security and Defense Issues?

	All Whites[a]	White GOP[b]	White Churchgoing GOP[c]	White Dem.[d]	All Blacks[e]
Democrat	17.4%	1.7%	0.8%	70.1%	67.3%
GOP	71.0%	92.3%	92.8%	13.4%	17.2%
Neither	7.9%	4.1%	4.8%	7.9%	10.1%
Both equally	3.6%	1.9%	1.6%	8.7%	5.4%

Source: Survey of Jacksonville Voters, 2004-2005. Public Opinion Research Laboratory, University of North Florida.
Note: All Whites vs. All Blacks significant at P ≤ .05 Chi^2 statistic.
[a] $N = 631$
[b] $N = 404$
[c] $N = 250$
[d] $N = 127$
[e] $N = 355$

Figure 4.4. Sign and message in front of the First Coast Conservative Baptist Church, in Jacksonville, Florida, July 2005. (Photo reproduced by permission of the *Florida Times-Union*.)

The data also show how unified Republicans are on moral and cultural issues. While such partisan support is to be expected, the extent of the support is striking. If Republicans can frame an issue as a moral, religious, or character issue, they can unify their party immediately.

National security and defense issues play important roles in this framing. Since the terrorist attacks of September 11, 2001, security issues have resumed importance among voters. The re-emergence of security issues has hurt Democrats in two ways. First, since the end of the Vietnam War, voters have viewed Democrats as being less supportive of the military than are Republicans. The war protests on college campuses became intertwined with other issues involved in the counterculture movements of the 1960s and 1970s. The emergence of a pro-peace candidate, George McGovern, in 1972 and the military cutbacks under Jimmy Carter in the late 1970s labeled Democrats as anti-military. In the South, where the military is revered and where many military bases are located, this label is a severe handicap for Democrats. Jacksonville itself is home to two major military bases. The military is a major economic contributor to the city.

Second, the ability of President George W. Bush and other Republicans to frame the war on terror as a moral contest further isolates Democrats in the South. President Bush's emphasis on "good" versus "evil" translates national security issues into moral and religious terms. In a speech at a pastor's conference, Jacksonville pastor Jerry Vines called the Muslim prophet Mohammed a "demon-possessed pedophile" (Pinzur 2002). Another pastor posted a message on a public church billboard proclaiming that Islam is evil. Jacksonville's other religious leaders distanced themselves from these statements, but the incidents highlight how, among some believers in the South, recent U.S. military involvement in the Middle East has taken on obvious religious overtones. Southern voters' powerful security concerns, combined with approval for the Republican Party's stances on religious issues, have strengthened the party's position in the region and the city. An overwhelming 71% of all white voters in Jacksonville believe that the Republican Party is stronger on national security and defense, in contrast with 17.4% of whites who trust the Democrats on this issue. This gap amounts to nearly 54 percentage points.

Republicans' huge advantage on the question of security and defense makes Democratic gains more difficult in an environment where national security and patriotism are concerns. As of this writing, backlash against the Iraq War is occurring among many voters across the nation, and this advantage is narrowing and may be disappearing. Yet, opposition against the Iraq War displays regional patterns as well. Southerners support the war at higher levels than do other Americans (Lester 2005). In summary, among many white voters in the South, Democrats are seen as less moral and less patriotic. This type of framing has important consequences for political leadership.

Consequences of Combining Religion and Politics

The clear nexus of religion and politics in the South has important consequences for the Republican leadership in the region. Four of these consequences are listed below.

The Growing Political and Social Influence of Churches Aids Republican Goals.

African American churches are the social and political centers for blacks in the South; white Protestant churches now have become social and political powers themselves. As previously stated, Protestant church leaders give political guidance in various ways, but their influence does not stop at suggesting which candidates to vote for or taking positions on issues. The very organizational structure of churches in the South has made government action less necessary and less wanted among some churchgoers.

Many white Protestant churches have replicated the black church model of pervasive church involvement in most aspects of their members' lives. In addition to mirroring the intertwining of religion, politics, and social support that took place during the civil rights era, this heavy involvement has other historical precedents as well. One parallel can be found in the relationship that developed between the Catholic Church and the great wave of Irish immigrants who fled to the United States during the Potato Famine of 1850. These immigrants received very little support from the U.S. government and from American society in general; as a result, Catholic parishes became the Irish immigrants' spiritual, social, and political centers. Food, fellowship, and even job assistance were offered to give these immigrants a safe place in a strange new land (Bankston and Hidalgo 2006). In many ways, conservative Christian churches in the South have adopted this model for their memberships.

Most Baptist and other evangelical churches offer help for family members, from infants to senior citizens. Within a single church, various ministries target separate demographic groups. Ministries may assist preschoolers, students, high-schoolers, single adults, divorced adults, military members, seniors, adult women, and women in general. The church functions as more than a once-a-week outlet; it becomes the social center of the lives of its members.

Members' heavy involvement with church-sponsored programs may have two impacts. First, members may not look to government for certain services because they already receive support from their church. Reliance on church ministries also may make members less supportive of government programs that offer similar services to citizens who do not have such a network of support. As shown in chapter 3, one of the major dividing lines between African Americans and whites in the South concerns the role of government in society. The strength of churches in the South creates another dividing line between citizens: those who make church the social and political center of their lives and those who do not. This reliance on church rather than the government aids Republicans because of the party's stated goal of lessening government influence in society. During the recent crisis in Jacksonville regarding the city's murder rate, the mayor did authorize more money for additional police officers, but his most visible action was to organize a "Day of Faith." At this gathering of 5,000 citizens, signs proclaimed that the city was "Arming Prayer Warriors" to confront the murder problem. Instead of widespread government action, the city's response to the rising murder rate was to literally pray for help and engage churches in the effort to spread nonviolence (Brumley 2006).

The second political impact caused by heavy involvement with churches is that the more a place of worship becomes central to citizens' lives, the more political influence pastors and church members have on one another. If beliefs expressed at church impact political beliefs, it follows that the more time one spends at church, the more entrenched one's beliefs become. These entrenched beliefs make it more difficult for a person to change opinions and partisan affiliations. This type of heavy involvement will undoubtedly continue and thus may make white Christian conservatives the bedrock of the Republican Party for years to come. For years, Republicans have wondered how African Americans have stayed loyal to the Democratic Party. Thirty years from now, Democrats may wonder how white churchgoers have remained such an important part of the Republican coalition.

Political Views Forged by Religious Values Make Compromise Difficult.

Since many religious voters view the world in a particular way, the chances for compromise about certain issues are slim. Compromise is central to the American political system. The founders created a system of government

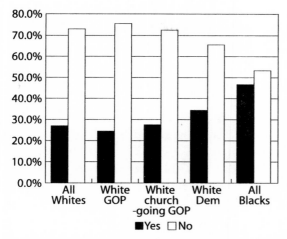

Figure 4.5. Bar chart of racial and church-attendance breakdown of responses to the question, "Do you believe the [opposite of respondent's] political party is sinful?" Survey of Jacksonville Voters, 2004–2005, Public Opinion Research Laboratory at the University of North Florida, $N = 948$.

that checks power throughout government. These checks make it difficult for government to do almost anything without compromise. In fact, the creation of the United States government itself was a compromise. Legislators must compromise with one another to get legislation passed. Presidents cannot pass laws on their own, so they must compromise with the legislature to pass new initiatives. Federal courts have the power of judicial review but the courts depend on elected officials to abide by the rule of law. In this framework, some understanding exists that political opponents must be part of creating and implementing public policy.

The close connection between religion and politics that many Jacksonville voters want could be a positive development for the political system. A greater emphasis on morality and religion in politics might lead to a more ethical political system. Such an emphasis might lead to elected officials telling the truth about the challenges the public must face. Even in the midst of historic economic growth, poverty still persists in many Southern areas, including cities such as Jacksonville. Since Christians dominate the religious makeup of the South, a new commitment to social and economic justice could result from a connection between religion and politics.

In 2003, Republican governor Bob Riley of Alabama tried to make this connection. He said that the taxes imposed on the poor in his state were "immoral." Thus, he advocated a $1.2 billion tax plan that would eliminate taxes for the poor and place more taxes on corporate interests such as timber. Riley told Alabama voters that it was their moral duty to take care of the poor (Reeves 2003). His initiative was defeated by a 2–1 margin. Few other Democrats or Republicans in the region have tried to translate religious beliefs into political action for the poor. This is an especially noticeable failure on the part of Democrats.

Another potential benefit of mixing religion and politics would be an emphasis on ethical and moral conduct, which could lead to better political campaigns. Attack ads that distort the truth would not pass these standards of religious morality.

Another positive development might be increased racial cooperation. Since a majority of blacks and whites believes firmly in the connection between religion and politics, such an agreement could be the basis for agreements on other issues. Such an emphasis on moral values might help bridge the serious racial divide that has haunted the South since the end of the Civil War. Several faith-based charities in Jacksonville have successfully made this connection.

Yet, the actual results of mixing politics and religion in Jacksonville and other Southern cities have been quite different. Clearly, this emphasis on morality and religion is being used to divide, not unify, Southerners. Rather than drawing on moral and religious arguments to face political issues (such as better education) that have widespread support among Southerners, politicians are using these arguments to focus on more divisive issues such as gay marriage and abortion. Partisan consultants use these issues to draw clear contrasts between candidates and parties. If someone does not agree with a party's moral position, then he or she must be immoral. Similarly, secular Democrats have weakened their cause by ignoring the fact that most Southerners are religious and by refusing to comment about the moral direction of the nation. Democrats may not agree with the positions held by religious voters, but in recent years they have made little effort to understand their concerns. For a party that lays claim to the mantle of Martin Luther King Jr., this lack of a moral dimension in politics is curious.

The infusion of evangelical religion into politics makes compromise difficult, if not impossible. Figure 4.5 shows how pervasive this mixing of religion, politics, and partisanship has become.

Almost one-third of whites and half of African Americans believe that the opposing party is not just wrong but *sinful*. It is difficult for parties to come together on issues when significant percentages of their followers believe that the other side is a sinner. Even a noncontroversial issue such as building bridges and roads becomes more difficult if political opponents are viewed in such a damning context. Indeed, compromise itself, the bedrock of the American political system, becomes a sin. In a worst-case scenario, entrenched religious and political beliefs could potentially fracture American society, just as religious and ethnic conflicts have done for other nations in recent history.

The Conflict of Economic Growth and Religious Beliefs

The views of conservative religious voters can conflict with some ingredients that are necessary to achieve economic growth in the twenty-first century. Employees with a church-centered life offer their employers attractive characteristics such as stable family lives and being active participants in the community. In past centuries, the famous Protestant work ethic helped the United States become an economic superpower (Ferguson 2003). Yet an active political agenda from churches also offers challenges to economic development.

After the Civil War, the South slowly shifted from an agrarian-dominated economy to a more broad-based manufacturing and service economy. Over the last 30 years, the U.S. and Southern economies have experienced another fundamental shift in development. The wealth of this new economy takes place in the sectors of technology, biomedical research, and service/entertainment. Chapter 5 will examine the political impacts of some of these changes. The fundamental change in the American economy over the last 40 years has put some religious beliefs and economic growth on a collision course.

For example, more Jacksonville residents support teaching creationism in public schools than do those who support teaching evolution. The recent arguments about intelligent design highlight this conflict. Supporters argue that evolution is just one of many theories about the origins of life. Critics of intelligent design argue that this approach is an attack on the scientific method itself. If school boards in the region try to pursue this controversy, it may send the unintended signal to businesses and researchers that the region is anti-science. In today's world economy, foreign investors and businesses want the latest technological knowledge and scientific advances. Evolution theory also is the basis for many important advances in physics and other scientific endeavors. If Southerners become bogged down in a debate that was addressed in the courts more than 80 years ago, international economic opportunities may go elsewhere.

Biomedical research is another important part of the new economy. Christian conservatives have taken a strong stance against stem-cell research and certain types of genetic research. If political leaders follow the cues of Christian conservative leaders, these types of industries may avoid setting up shop in the South. Medical research is critical to the economies of many states, and this type of research may be on a collision course with the conservative makeup of the region.

Finally, since more of the U.S. economy has become service- and tourism-oriented, some of these related industries may run afoul of the mores of Southerners. For instance, church leaders in Jacksonville have continually blocked efforts to build a large entertainment area downtown because it would be home to additional establishments that serve alcohol. Leisure travel is an important part of the economies of many Southern states. Locations that vie for vacation dollars have to offer many different forms of recreation. While successful family-centered destinations such as Disney World comply in most respects with traditional Southern standards, other types of leisure activity are not compatible with the beliefs of conservative Christians. Even places like Disney World can arouse controversy among conservative Christians regarding issues like same-sex marriage benefits for their employees. Before Hurricane Katrina, gambling was an important economic resource for Mississippi and Alabama. Places such as Savannah, Georgia; Myrtle Beach, South Carolina; and Daytona Beach, Florida are known for their party nightlife. Some locations in the South will have to decide whether to worship the vacation dollar or stay with their conservative beliefs. For the Republican Party, these conflicts will pit their voting base of Christian conservatives against their financial base of economic conservatives.

Conclusion

In sum, the rise of the Republicans has impacted the difficult relationship between religion and politics in the area. The important political influence of conservative Protestant churches and Catholic churches in the Republican Party has helped to mobilize churchgoing whites. In general, African American voters still view their churches as sources of political guidance. Since religious beliefs are particularly intense and consistent, the increased political activity of white churches has added another dynamic to the relationship between whites and blacks in the South. Since the end of the Civil War, religious worship in Jacksonville has been a source of racial segregation. Churches are now sources of political segregation as well, with Democrats dominating black churches and Republicans attending white churches. This phenomenon adds another layer of political separation between blacks and whites. Although blacks and whites who regularly attend church agree on many social issues, there is stark disagreement relating to economic issues and national security. Thus, black and white churches are centers of organization for competing political parties.

The prominence of conservative white churches in the Republican Party has brought different types of issues to the political forefront. Many Jacksonville political candidates describe themselves as pro-life and anti-abortion. For example, the Duval County School Board authorized an expensive federal court fight to protect prayer before high school graduations. Gay marriage has been condemned by several religious leaders in the area. Without the activism of churches and church leaders, these issues might not assume such a high profile in the city. The mixture of strong religious beliefs and political action can make political compromise more difficult. New Republican leadership has made the discussion of religious beliefs and moral issues much more prevalent in the public arena.

5

Economic Change

"It's business friendly" (Basch 2004, B2). These words were spoken by the chairman of a Fortune 500 company who decided to relocate his company to Jacksonville, Florida, in 2003. Fidelity National, a leading firm that processes mortgages and offers title insurance, was looking for a community with a welcoming business environment as well as lower housing and construction costs. The company was leaving California with its heavy regulations and higher taxes. The short phrase "business friendly" sums up the economic appeal of the South. Most parts of the region have low taxes and few regulations and are not heavily unionized. These policies and circumstances have helped to make the South the fastest-growing economic region in the nation. Job growth in the South has outpaced that in all other regions in the country by 40% over the last 20 years (Dodson et al. 2004). This economic growth also has spurred population growth.

While the region's economy has expanded, poverty and racial disparities in income still plague both rural and metropolitan areas in the South. Nearly 20% of Southern children grow up in a household with an annual income below the poverty line (Dodson et al. 2004). Many rural communities in the region still deal with persistent poverty. In *Dismantling Persistent Poverty in the Southeastern United States,* researchers from the Carl Vinson Institute concluded that more than half of the consistently poor counties in the United States are in the South (Ledbetter 2004). In one Alabama county, every child in public school comes from a family that lives in poverty (Associated Press 2005). The devastating impacts of Hurricane Katrina in 2005 highlighted that Southern poverty impacts blacks and other minorities in disproportionate numbers. While new migrants to the region from the Northeast and Midwest usually fill high-skill jobs, many native Southerners are stuck in low-wage occupations. Low tax rates in some Southern states translate into minimal investments in education and job training. If these trends continue, the South could become home to the richest and the poorest citizens in the country. Such an income gap could have profound effects on the region's new political structure.

The South's recent economic growth would have been unthinkable 70 years ago. In the late 1930s, President Franklin Roosevelt identified the South's weak economy as the largest domestic problem faced by the United States (Scher 1997). The region's economic misery rested on a lasting and pervasive historical foundation. The Civil War had left the region devastated both socially and economically. The economy of the post-Civil War South was a literal disaster. The postwar South had little capital to start or expand businesses. Moreover, demand was plummeting for its largest export, cotton. It was still an agricultural region in a nation that was moving beyond farming as its main economic activity (Foner 1988).

Industrialization came to the South after the Civil War, but the conditions of this industrialization did not necessarily create economic wealth. Well into the 1900s, industries came to the South for cheap labor and minimal regulations. In his important overview of Southern poverty, Richard Scher (1997, 24) notes that "Southern industry provided almost exclusively low skill, low wage jobs . . . . little protection for workers existed and virtually no unionization occurred." Most industries were owned by non-Southerners, and companies made little investment to improve the quality of the Southern workforce. These miserable economic conditions impacted the vast majority of Southerners. Millions of African Americans migrated to the North to find better social and economic opportunities. Those Southerners who stayed, like the white mill workers, were labeled "cheap and contented" for having adapted to their limited prospects (Lewis 1929). Economic and political power was firmly entrenched in the hands of a few white elites.

As poverty remained throughout the region, some Southern states became receptive to the idea of economic populism. Huey Long, the legendary Louisiana governor, became a national force during the Depression by advocating an aggressive government plan to redistribute wealth in the country. Most of the South accepted Roosevelt's New Deal, but looked warily at aspects of federal involvement. Some Southern governors refused to apply federal wage guidelines under the New Deal to blacks in the region (Brattain 2002). This difficult time was critical because it forced most Southern leaders to actively recruit economic opportunities. The South was going to become "business friendly" because it had no choice.

Among the major contributors to manufacturing employment in the South was the textile industry. Jobs in textile manufacturing were difficult, with low wages and few safety regulations. Unionization slowly worked its way into Southern manufacturing but its ultimate impact varied by location and circumstance. Many local unions would not admit blacks into their ranks, thus limiting their bargaining power (Halpern 1997).

The post–World War II economy offered new opportunities to the South. During the war, the South was involved in a huge military buildup, and many of the military bases that were enhanced or created for the war endured as permanent fixtures in the region. Improvements in communications and transportation made it much easier for other parts of the country to interact with the South. A middle class was emerging, but low-wage jobs still remained a stubborn trait of the Southern economy. In 1950, nearly 40% of the nation's workers were unionized; in the South, the number was 17% (Simon 1997).

An important change took place in the latter part of the twentieth century when most of the South's economic activity shifted from rural to metropolitan areas. Economic diversification became the key characteristic of the Southern economy. Today the region's economic cornerstones are banking and finance. The nation's largest banking chain is located in Charlotte, North Carolina. With improved transportation throughout the region, the real estate and construction industries have become central to the economy. Jacksonville, Savannah, Charleston, Miami, and Norfolk are major ports for commercial shipping. Atlanta, Georgia, now has the nation's busiest airport and is home to the headquarters of companies such as Coca Cola and Home Depot. Although recent military base closures have hurt some areas of the South, buildup and support for the wars in Iraq and Afghanistan have aided the economy. The region's warm climate has spawned a growth in tourism and service industries in most Southern states. The increasing population keeps these industries expanding.

Globalization has offered mixed results for the region. Companies have moved many industries to nations with lower wages and easy regulations. Nations such as Mexico, India, and China have done to the Southern United States what the South did to the North for two generations: offer U.S. companies a workforce with low wages and few legal regulations. Textile industries have been hit particularly hard. South Carolina alone lost 76,000 manufacturing jobs between 2000 and 2005 (Associated Press 2005). Yet, along with having funneled some jobs overseas, the dynamics of the worldwide economy also have introduced new industries to the South. Technology companies have located throughout the region due to lower living costs for their employees. Biomedical industries also have found a home in several Southern states, including North Carolina, Florida, and Georgia. Auto manufacturers still are more likely to locate new plants in the South than in other areas of the country.

Employees of growing Southern industries and businesses have transformed Southern politics. Black and Black (2000) emphasize the importance of white middle class voters to the Republican Party. Until the latter part of the twentieth century, the South had only a small middle class. These new middle class voters are much more amenable to the appeal of the Republican Party, which promises smaller government and more tax cuts. These Southerners fail to see many benefits coming to them from the federal government so they are much less likely to want to fund government programs. Many of these middle class and upper class voters have settled in suburbs where they are separated from the poverty of both the rural and urban South. As Black and Black (2000, 5) note, "Many of these upwardly mobile individuals, wanting to keep the lion's share of the earnings, view the Republicans as far more sympathetic than the Democrats to their economic interests."

While Democrats have been hit hard by the influx of Republican-leaning middle class whites, the party's most difficult challenge has been the slow erosion of support from the white working class. The Democratic Party came to dominance in the 1930s by putting together a broad coalition of Northern blacks, union workers, Southern whites, and new immigrants. While these groups shared few social or cultural concerns, they came together politically due to common economic interests. The Democratic Party was the party of the working class; this economic appeal was the party's foundation. Working-class whites have been slower to move to the Republican Party than have other income groups, but they have moved (Meyerson 2005). The current lack of support from working-class whites, especially men, in some of the poorest counties in the nation is a direct assault on the efficacy of the Democratic Party in the South. These working-class whites are the important economic group for Democrats to try to win back.

Jacksonville's Economy

Jacksonville is the largest single-city entity in Florida. According to the U.S. Department of Labor, median family income is more than $56,000 in the Northeast Florida area (Jacksonville Community Council Inc. 2005). The St. Johns River, which runs through downtown Jacksonville, has been a source of economic activity since the city's founding. The city has two major mili-

Table 5.1. Jacksonville MSA Nonagricultural Employment by Sector

Construction	39,700	6.8%
Manufacturing	36,200	6.2%
Trade, transportation, & utilities	127,500	21.6%
Information	11,300	1.9%
Financial activities	58,100	10.0%
Professional & business services	88,100	15.2%
Education & health services	67,700	11.7%
Leisure & hospitality	55,800	9.6%
Other services	26,600	4.5%
Government	69,700	12.0%

Source: Jacksonville Regional Chamber of Commerce 2004.

tary bases, and the military provides the largest number of jobs from any one sector of the economy. Other key industries include financial services, real-estate development and construction, and medical services. Table 5.1 offers a breakdown of employment by sector.

Jacksonville and other places in Florida have been able to weather recent recessions due to this diversification. Yet, these sectors also point to a stark fact. New jobs generally fall into two categories: low-level service jobs and

Figure 5.1. Downtown Jacksonville, Florida, February 2005. (Photo reproduced by permission of the *Florida Times Union*.)

Figure 5.2. Navy P-3 military aircraft flies over Interstate 95 in Jacksonville, Florida, May 2005. (Photo reproduced by permission of the *Florida Times-Union.*)

jobs that require high levels of education and skills. Allen Greenspan, the former chairman of the Board of Governors of the Federal Reserve, testified in 2005 about the increasing dangers posed by the widening income gap in the nation. This gap may be more prominent in the South due to the region's long history of poverty (Hill 2005). This gap is apparent in Jacksonville. Thousands of new high-skill jobs have been created there in the last two decades, but the city's per capita income as a percentage of national income has declined over the last 15 years. Especially acute is the gap between white and black residents. Per capita income of white residents is 47% higher than that of blacks (Conrad 2005).

Increased mobility and ease of access to transportation have widened the income gap. No longer is Jacksonville dominated by native residents. The South in general is expanding, with 10,000 new residents arriving every year. Some of these residents come from other parts of the country, but

Table 5.2. How Long Have You Lived in Jacksonville?

Less than 1 year	2.0%
1 to 5 years	13.7%
6 to 10 years	10.6%
11 to 20 years	17.8%
More than 20 years	32.2%
Native of Jacksonville	23.7%

Source: Survey of Jacksonville Voters, 2004-2005. Public Opinion Research Laboratory, University of North Florida.
Note: N = 948.

Table 5.3. In Which Region of the Country Did You Live When You Were Six Years Old?

South	59.4%
Northeast	20.8%
Midwest	11.8%
Central Plains	0.6%
Mountain West	0.3%
West Coast	2.4%
Other	4.6%

Source: Survey of Jacksonville Voters, 2004–2005. Public Opinion Research Laboratory, University of North Florida.
Note: N = 945.

Table 5.4. Income and Political Party Identification of Jacksonville Respondents

	Less than $20K[a]	$20K to $50K[b]	$50K to $100K[c]	More than $100K[d]
Democrats	44.2%	39.9%	32.8%	26.3%
Republicans	36.4%	43.8%	52.4%	57.5%
Independents	11.7%	10.9%	8.1%	9.4%
Other	7.8%	5.4%	6.6%	6.9%

Source: Survey of Jacksonville Voters, 2004-2005. Public Opinion Research Laboratory, University of North Florida.
Notes:
[a] N = 77
[b] N = 258
[c] N = 332
[d] N = 160

many come from other parts of the South. The new Southerners have helped transform the region both economically and politically.

Generally, these new Southerners are younger and have higher levels of education than do native residents. They have added to the upper middle class and thus have helped Republicans. Table 5.4 illustrates the importance of income to party identification.

As expected, as income rises, so does Republican identification. The upper-middle class ($50,000–$100,000) has a Republican bias, but it is not overwhelming. The working class and the lower-middle class (below $50,000) have a strong Democratic advantage. These data indicate that the party of the New Deal still resonates with lower-income Southerners.

Yet, examine table 5.5. When race is introduced into the comparisons, the Democratic advantage among lower-income whites vanishes. This is a serious dilemma for Democrats. The inability to attract lower-income to middle-income whites has hurt the party. In the Jacksonville 2003 mayoral election, the winning Republican candidate was able to sweep much of the city's west side, where many working-class whites reside. Map 7 reveals that the inner core of the city with its low-income residents supports Democrats.

Table 5.5. Political Party Identification and Income of Whites and Blacks in Jacksonville

	Whites				Blacks			
	Less than $20K[a]	$20K to $50K[b]	$50K to $100K[c]	More than $100K[d]	Less than $20K[e]	$20K to $50K[f]	$50K[b] to $100K[g]	More than $100K[h]
Democrat	17.5%	20.5%	22.0%	18.5%	88.6%	88.5%	78.3%	70.0%
Republican	65.0%	62.0%	64.5%	66.2%	2.9%	3.8%	12.2%	13.3%
Independent	12.5%	13.9%	7.8%	9.2%	4.3%	3.1%	4.3%	13.3%
Other	5.0%	3.6%	5.7%	6.2%	4.3%	4.6%	5.2%	3.3%

Source: Survey of Jacksonville Voters, 2004-2005. Public Opinion Research Laboratory, University of North Florida.

Notes:

[a] $N = 40$

[b] $N = 166$

[c] $N = 245$

[d] $N = 130$

[e] $N = 70$

[f] $N = 130$

[g] $N = 115$

[h] $N = 30$

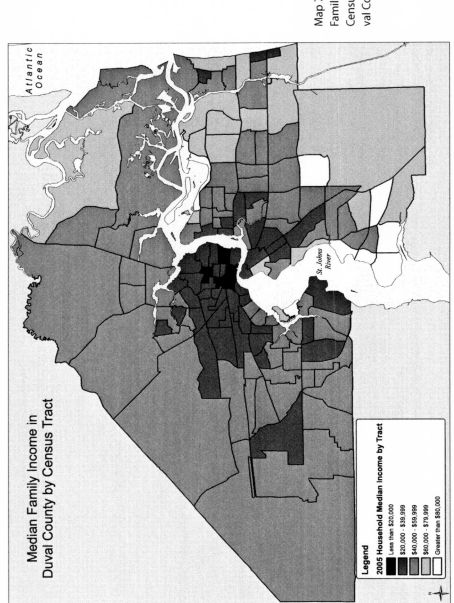

Map 7. Median Family Income by Census Tract in Duval County, Florida.

Table 5.6. Blacks' Income and Political Party Identification

	Less than $50K[a]	$50K or above[b]
Democrat	88.5%	76.6%
Republican	3.5%	12.4%
Independent	3.5%	6.2%
Other	4.5%	4.8%

Source: Survey of Southern Voters, June 2004. Public Opinion Research Laboratory, University of North Florida.
Note: P ≤ .05 chi^2 statistic.
[a] $N = 200$
[b] $N = 145$

Yet the city's west side, which has a substantial lower-middle class, has gone solidly Republican in recent years.

Analysts differ on how to define the working class (Yglesias 2006). Some define the class by education and others by income level. For the data presented in tables 5.4 and 5.5, two categories are used to capture the working class. These categories are family income below $20,000, to represent those in poverty, and family income from $20,000–$50,000, to represent the lower middle class. After a first descriptive look at these data, these two categories are then combined to make comparisons more meaningful due to the small sample size in the below-$20,000 category. For African Americans, the data are separated into two income categories.

Again, African American loyalty to the Democratic Party is apparent. As expected, nearly 90% of blacks with a family income of less than $50,000 are Democrats, as shown in table 5.6. This loyalty makes it imperative for Democrats to talk about issues concerning economic justice. With a disproportionate share of African Americans in lower-income categories, economic issues may be more important to many blacks than to most whites.

Higher-income blacks also are generally in the Democratic column, but the data indicate that more than 10% identify themselves as Republican. Due to the larger margin of error associated with a subgroup, these results are not conclusive; however, this pattern is potentially significant. If Republicans could attract 10%–15% of higher-income blacks, Democrats would be in serious trouble since the Democratic Party now counts on 85%–90% support among Southern blacks. Anecdotal evidence suggests that some higher-income blacks are trending Republican. In Jacksonville, a state legislator and two city council members are black Republicans, and they were

Table 5.7. In Disputes between Businesses and Labor Unions, Do You Usually Support the Business or the Labor Union?

	Whites			Blacks	
	Less than $50K[a]	$50K to $100K[b]	$100K or more[c]	Less than $50K[d]	More than $50K[e]
Businesses	52.3%	55.0%	66.9%	23.0%	25.7%
Labor unions	36.7%	35.8%	22.3%	71.2%	68.1%
Neither	11.1%	9.2%	10.7%	5.8%	6.3%

Source: Survey of Southern Voters, June 2004. Public Opinion Research Laboratory, University of North Florida.
Notes: [a] N = 199.
[b] N = 229
[c] N =121
[d] N = 191
[e] N = 144

elected in overwhelmingly white areas. This small potential change in black support for the Democratic Party is important only because of how badly Democrats are doing among white working-class and middle-class voters.

Republican support for businesses offers a political advantage. Probusiness sentiment is apparent among Jacksonville voters. A strong majority recognizes that the city is a good place to run a business. When respondents were asked whether they favored unions or businesses in labor disputes, the pro-business trend was clear among whites in table 5.7.

These data highlight an obvious problem for Democrats. Democrats have long been associated with organized labor. Yet unionization in the South has always been low. Support for unions was the one way that Democrats could show their allegiance to the blue-collar workforce. Yet with membership and support for unions at a historic low, this allegiance to unions has a much smaller impact.

Support for efforts to assist the lower-middle class and the working class with large-scale federal assistance is complicated by suspicion of federal government programs. The data in table 5.8 show that state government is favored when white respondents are asked to compare state and federal governments.

Inherent distrust of large government programs hurts Democrats who are trying to put together a coherent strategy to attract the economic vote. Republicans have campaigned on the idea that they are the party of states'

Table 5.8. Which Level of Government Would You Choose to Handle Important Political Issues that Matter to You?

	Whites			Blacks	
	Less than $50K[a]	$50K to $100K[b]	$100K or more[c]	Less than $50K[d]	More than $50K[e]
Federal	33.0%	36.3%	28.3%	56.4%	43.0%
State	61.6%	59.1%	68.3%	42.5%	53.3%
Local	5.4%	4.7%	3.3%	1.1%	3.7%

Source: Survey of Southern Voters, June 2004. Public Opinion Research Laboratory, University of North Florida.
Note: Less than $50K vs. More than $50K for Blacks significant at $P \leq .05$ chi^2 statistic.
[a] $N = 185$
[b] $N = 215$
[c] $N = 120$
[d] $N = 179$
[e] $N = 135$

rights and small government. While not always used in practice, these ideas are viewed as being more attractive than are Washington-based solutions.

Parties in the United States have usually been separated along economic interests and groups. Thomas Jefferson became a Democrat (an anti-Federalist) because he believed that John Adams was fixated on helping merchants and other business interests at the expense of rural interests. Andrew Jackson implemented his form of Jacksonian democracy so the common man would have a voice in government. The Civil War separated the Democratic and Republican parties into distinct economic camps. The post-Reconstruction South dominated by Democrats had little in common economically with the industrial North. The New Deal in the 1930s defined Democrats as the party that would use the national government to make conditions better for the working class and the poor. Republicans were the party of businesses and corporations who stood against massive government intervention. In sum, if there ever was a clear dividing line between the Democratic and Republican parties, economic status was it.

Yet, this dividing line for whites in the South is gone. Table 5.9 examines voters' attitudes about which party better represents the working class.

Among those whites earning less than $50,000, neither party is strongly favored as best representing the interests of working people. That Democrats have no clear advantage on this question again highlights how images

Table 5.9. Which Political Party Better Represents the Interests of Working People?

	Whites			Blacks	
	Less than $50K[a]	$50K to $100K[b]	More than $100K[c]	Less than $50K[d]	More than $100K[f]
Democratic	41.0%	41.6%	38.2%	86.7%	81.1%
Republican	44.9%	49.4%	48.0%	6.6%	10.5%
Neither	8.3%	4.7%	8.9%	2.6%	7.7%
Both equally	5.9%	4.3%	4.9%	4.1%	0.7%

Source: Survey of Jacksonville Voters, 2004-2005. Public Opinion Research Laboratory, University of North Florida.
Note: Blacks' data significant at $P \leq .05$ chi^2 statistic.
[a] $N = 205$
[b] $N = 233$
[c] $N = 123$
[d] $N = 196$
[e] $N = 113$
[f] $N = 29$

Table 5.10. Which Political Party Better Represents the Interests of Working People?

	All Whites			Churchgoing Whites		
	Less than $50K[a]	$50K to $100K[b]	More than $100K[c]	Less than $50K[d]	$50K to $100K[e]	More than $100K[f]
Democratic	41.0%	41.6%	38.2%	31.7%	33.9%	37.0%
Republican	44.9%	49.4%	48.0%	58.7%	55.4%	46.6%
Neither	8.3%	4.7%	8.9%	4.8%	5.8%	11.0%
Both equally	5.9%	4.3%	4.9%	4.8%	5.0%	5.5%

Source: Survey of Jacksonville Voters, 2004-2005. Public Opinion Research Laboratory, University of North Florida.
Notes:
[a] $N = 205$
[b] $N = 233$
[c] $N = 123$
[d] $N = 104$
[e] $N = 121$
[f] $N = 73$

Table 5.11. Which Political Party Helps the Middle Class More?

	Whites			Blacks	
	Less than $50K[a]	$50K to $100K[b]	$100K or more[c]	$50K or less[d]	More than $50K[e]
Democratic	28.1%	30.6%	26.8%	68.3%	70.8%
Republican	58.6%	57.9%	59.3%	25.7%	23.6%
Neither	8.9%	6.8%	8.1%	2.5%	3.5%
Both equally	4.4%	4.7%	5.7%	3.5%	2.1%

Source: Survey of Southern Voters, June 2004. Public Opinion Research Laboratory, University of North Florida.

Notes:
[a] $N = 203$
[b] $N = 235$
[c] $N = 123$
[d] $N = 202$
[e] $N = 144$

of the parties have been transformed. Simply put, if Democrats are not recognized as representing the working class, whom do they represent?

The important connection between religion and politics also may play a role. Perhaps Democrats' economic appeal is limited because Southern voters' minds are on other matters. Examining support for the working class by church attendance shows that Republicans may enhance their economic appeal with whites who attend church. Lower-income churchgoing whites are much less likely to view Democrats as the protectors of the working class. Again, with hundreds of churches in the area, moral issues may trump economics for many Jacksonville residents. As n   tioned in a previous chapter, one Jacksonville pastor encouraged his followers to forget about economics and focus on moral values when voting. If many Southerners follow admonitions like this, a major attraction of the Democratic Party will be lost.

This trend continues when perceptions about representing the middle class are examined. In table 5.11, when asked which party helps the middle class more, all income groups among whites gave a clear answer: Republicans.

In the 1990s, President Bill Clinton made helping the middle class one of his primary political themes. With rising health care costs, the loss of pensions, and stagnant wages, middle-class concerns were supposed to be priorities for Democrats. Yet, in 2004, Stanley Greenburg, Clinton's former pollster, argued that "Democrats forgot the middle class" (Greenberg 2005, 7). Not only do upper-middle-class voters think that the Republican Party is the party of the middle class, but so do white working-class voters. Thus, voters who hope to improve their economic fortunes are casting their votes for Republicans. These data indicate that in Republican-leaning areas, the white middle-class has gone and stayed Republican. If Republicans can keep the entrepreneurial white middle class, their political standing will only strengthen.

Consequences of Economic Change

Republicans Benefit from Current Economic Trends.

In recent years, the economy of the South has benefitted from the probusiness attitudes of its residents and leaders. Due to the history of economic scarcity in the South, many of the region's state governments enticed businesses by offering land, low taxes, right-to-work laws, and fewer regulations. Many of these policies already were in place when Democrats dominated the region. Yet, since the emergence of the Republican Party in the region, conservative economic attitudes now have a home in a conservative political party. Since competition to attract businesses is on a worldwide level, Southern Republicans will continue to be explicitly probusiness. This reputation is a plus in attracting new industries and their employees to the Republican Party.

Republican Philosophy Does Not Address Poverty.

The emphasis on attracting high-wage industries and jobs benefits Republicans with voters from the upper-middle class and upper classes, but it does not address the long-term plague of Southern poverty. The region's new economic order created two categories of job opportunities: high-skilled jobs that require advanced levels of education or training and service-industry jobs that are low skill and offer low wages. Migration from other areas of the United States has shown that the South can attract highly skilled employees to fill high-wage jobs. Yet, uncertainty exists about the Republican Party's ability to address rural and urban poverty, a poverty that is concentrated among native Southerners. Conservatives have criticized federal poverty programs, especially those of the Great Society, for having contributed to poverty, not alleviating it.

Yet, if Republicans continue their dominance in the South, will Republicans from the federal government on down try to address poverty? No apparent strategy exists. Attitudes about small government and low taxes make it difficult for Republicans to put together a coherent strategy. As a result of low taxes, spending in the South on education and training lags behind that of other regions of the country. It is difficult for many Southern states to make long-term investments in education when they are struggling to meet the challenges of current growth. Low tax revenues force many states to look to the federal government when trying to address poverty and working-class issues. Yet, if Republicans remain in power at the presidential level, a federal response to poverty is unlikely.

In Jacksonville, two Republican mayors have taken a proactive approach to urban poverty. One program in 1995 focused on neighborhoods in crisis. In these "Intensive Care Neighborhoods," condemned buildings were removed, streets were paved and cleaned, and a range of government services were made available to residents (Bauerlein 1998). This successful program helped six neighborhoods in crisis.

The current Republican mayor has put together a comprehensive examination of the wage gap in Jacksonville. This examination is called *Blueprint for Prosperity* (Conrad 2005). The goal of this blueprint is "Raising the Income per Capita in Duval County." This plan warns that if income disparities are not addressed, negative consequences will occur in the next 30 years, including: 1) larger disparities between black and white residents; 2) a higher poverty rate; 3) a higher murder rate; and 4) a lower standard of living for county residents (Conrad 2005, 5).

Both of these efforts are forward thinking, but the long structural history of Southern poverty requires a more comprehensive effort. Local governments cannot address these major problems on their own. All of these challenges require substantial investments over the long-term from local, state, and national governments. Such a coordinated effort is not apparent as of this writing.

Lack of a Democratic Economic Strategy

Democrats built their political success in the twentieth century by responding to the excesses of industrial capitalism. Addressing issues such as the minimum wage, collective bargaining, and worker safety offered strong political benefits to Democrats. However, the service-dominated economy of the world in the twenty-first century is not adaptable to long-established

Democratic views of regulation, worker protection, and support for unions. The more regulations that are placed on businesses in the United States, the more likely it is that additional businesses will move overseas. If Democrats attempt to block expanded worldwide trade, some workers may be protected, but others will be hurt by businesses' inability to sell goods overseas, which cuts into job opportunities at ports and import/export centers. For example, Jacksonville is home to a major port, which offers some of the best blue-collar jobs in the city. Protectionist policies would undoubtedly result in fewer jobs for Jacksonville port workers.

Moreover, Democratic programs that have been successful in confronting poverty have since been adopted by the Republican Party. These programs include Social Security and Medicare, which have done more to alleviate poverty among senior citizens than any government initiatives in the history of the United States. The long-term costs of these programs are formidable. Yet, both Democrats and Republicans support the continuation and even the expansion of these programs. President George W. Bush signed into law a Medicare prescription drug benefit in 2004. These programs are so expensive and consume so much of the federal budget that bold new and long-term initiatives to address poverty are unlikely to be launched in the near future.

Accordingly, Democrats have little to offer in terms of economic assistance. Unions have never had widespread popularity in the South, and membership is declining. Under current fiscal realities, no money is available for new wide-ranging programs that address those in poverty. Increased regulations on businesses may help employees in the short run but may become limiting and unrealistic in the context of a competitive worldwide economy. There are no arrows left in the current Democratic quiver. This dynamic must change for Democrats to become viable again in the region.

In sum, Republican leadership matters in Jacksonville and the South because it matches the pro-business political party with a pro-business region of the United States. Republican political leaders will continue to aggressively seek new economic opportunities through tax incentives and less burdensome regulatory schemes. These strategies bode well for well-educated and skilled Southerners. Yet, the emergence of Republican leadership may make it difficult to address issues such as the large wage gap and poverty. The catastrophe of Hurricane Katrina offered a unique opportunity to address race-based poverty. President Bush in his speech from New Orleans after the storm pledged to deal with the legacy of poverty and race. Yet Congress and the president did little to bring these ideas to fruition (Alter 2006).

In short, Republican leaders are natural allies with businesses, but they will have a much more difficult time providing innovative policies to address the income gap.

Conclusion

When V. O. Key examined the South more than 50 years ago, he found a region with a stagnant political system. These politics included one-party domination held together by racial segregation. Key found that this system had dire consequences for both the economic and democratic development of the region.

The South of the twenty-first century is quite different. Two political parties are established and competitive, although Republicans have moved into a majority position in many places. The civil rights movement of the 1960s has given rise to active black political involvement. African Americans hold more than 5,000 elected positions in the region, mostly in African American areas. The region's current economic growth is stunning, especially compared to that of the 1930s, when President Roosevelt called the South the "nation's number one economic problem." A thriving middle class has led the Southern economic transformation. Examples of these changes and advances can be found in the city of Jacksonville, Florida.

This book has posed the question: Do these political changes matter? The study finds that the way that Republicans have come to power in the region will have important consequences on future governance. By examining race, religion and economic change, the consequences of these political changes are apparent.

The Emergence of the Republican Party Has Combined Racial and Partisan Separation.

To a great extent, the political system of the South is still unwilling to confront racial differences and economic poverty. Different histories and economic positions have re-segregated Southern politics between blacks and whites. Generally, the Republican Party is the home of white conservatives while African Americans are the base of the Democratic Party. This voluntary political segregation allows race to continue to play a powerful role in the politics of the region. Republicans have little electoral incentive to address racial concerns because few blacks support the GOP. Moreover, Republicans do not favor large government domestic programs that could be employed to address racial disparities. Elected African Americans also have little incentive to constructively engage white Southerners on issues such as urban poverty. Most elected African Americans represent electoral areas that are majority black or have substantial black populations and do not need white votes for political survival. This insular black leadership has been criticized by many African Americans.

This type of political standoff has important impacts. After years of progress since the mid-1960s, attitudes of blacks and whites are *further* apart on racial issues than they were 15 years ago in Jacksonville (Jacksonville Community Council 2005). Clearly, living conditions have improved for most Southerners, both black and white, since the 1960s. Yet, there is wide variation associated with this economic progression. Gaps between blacks and whites in health and other social indicators are *increasing* 40 years after the civil rights movement. These large gaps are real threats to the economic and social stability of the city and the region. These trends were apparent prior to the rise of the Republican Party in the region and are not the result of Republican leadership. Yet confronting these issues under the current political system may be extremely difficult with most whites in one party and most African Americans in the other.

Party competition has not brought on some of the changes that V. O. Key envisioned. The addition of newly arrived Hispanic immigrants also will force Southerners to confront a new player in the racial dynamics of the South. Will these new Southerners be welcomed as a needed workforce for Southern businesses or will they be viewed as political and economic threats?

The Rise of the Republican Party in the Region Has Mobilized White Protestant and Catholic Churches to Be Active Participants in Electoral Politics.

Religious faith and church-centered activities also are prominent factors in modern Southern politics. The data presented make it clear that religious and moral issues are important to Southern voters. The examples in Jacksonville show the extent of the collaboration between churches and political activity. White Protestant and Catholic churches have adopted the tactics of black churches by encouraging members to connect their religious beliefs to political actions.

This connection appears deep-rooted and lasting, but the consequences of this nexus between religion and politics are uncertain. Essentially, candidates for office in the South have to pass a religious test before they are acceptable. If they do not pass this test, their opponents brand them as "liberal" and "immoral." This type of divisive rhetoric is potentially dangerous. Many Southern voters are already divided on racial lines; the addition of religion as a separating principle negatively impacts social cohesion. There is a big difference between moral certainty and political reality.

The introduction of morality to politics has not been used to address the most lasting legacy of Southern life: poverty. A Republican governor from Alabama tried this approach, but voters quickly rebuffed him. While poverty disproportionately impacts black citizens, there are millions of additional Southerners of all ethnic backgrounds who live in poverty. Republicans have been able to carry the white working-class vote without offering an economic policy that addresses their economic plight. Nor do Democrats have much to offer economically. Neither party appears to have a coherent policy to address the increasing income gap. The result is a region that vividly highlights a national trend: the growing separation between the upper and working classes. This trend is ominous because the South's startling economic success in recent years has been due to an expanding middle class. If the middle class disappears, politics in the South will be fundamentally transformed.

The New Political Order in the South Will Make the Region Even More Accommodating to Businesses; yet, the Wage Gap in the Region Will Likely Increase.

The advent of a new world economy that rewards specific skills and high levels of education puts the South at a crossroads. With political cooperation and the correct investments in education over the long term, the South could become the most prosperous region in the most prosperous nation in world history. Yet, if current trends persist, the South may one day resemble the struggling democracies of South America. This alternative would feature a disappearing middle class and huge gap of wealth between the rich and the poor. This increased poverty would only exacerbate tensions over racial and religious differences.

The Republican Party has become the dominant political party in a U.S. region that has had a tumultuous social and economic history. The transformation of the political system of the South will make it difficult to address the sad legacies of racial separation and economic poverty. History and the well-being of future Southerners await the outcome.

Appendix A

Methodology for Surveys

For the Southern survey, 803 interviews were conducted in February and March 2004 at the Public Opinion Research Laboratory at the University of North Florida, in Jacksonville. This survey was conducted through the use of Computer Assisted Telephone Interviewing (CATI) at a 27-station polling laboratory at the University of North Florida (UNF). A sample of the polling universe was selected through random-digit-dialing methodology. Interviewers were trained in survey methodology and were supervised during data collection. For noncompletes with a working residential phone line, at least six callbacks were attempted. To ensure a representative sample, calls were made from 5:00 p.m. to 9:00 p.m.. The screening questions asked if the voter had voted in the 2000 presidential election and was planning to vote in the 2004 presidential election. If the respondent answered yes to both questions, he or she was kept in the survey. Respondents were stratified by state, as described below:

States Surveyed:

1. Alabama	5%
2. Arkansas	3%
3. Florida	20%
4. Georgia	9%
5. Louisiana	5%
6. Mississippi	3%
7. North Carolina	10%
8. South Carolina	4%
9. Tennessee	7%
10. Texas	24%
11. Virginia	9%

The data are weighted by gender. Since sample statistics from this survey looked similar to those of other surveys of the South, further weighting was not done. For example, exit polls of Southern states during the 2000 presidential election showed party identification to be 40% Democrat, 38%

Republican, and 22% independent. The 2000 exit poll was used for comparison since the UNF poll was completed *before* the November 2004 election. This UNF survey had a party-identification breakdown of 36% Democrat, 36% Republican, and 23% Independent. These numbers also were similar to the 2001 Odum Institute's Southern Focus Poll, which had a partisan breakdown of 34% Democrat, 34% Republican, and 22% Independent/Other. The Odum Institute poll is available online at http://www.irss.unc.edu/irss/home.asp.

The results presented in the book do not include the responses of Don't Know or Refused, unless otherwise indicated. Assuming no nonrandom error, the margin of error for the entire Southern sample is +/- 3.5%. The margin of error for subgroups can range from +/-4.7% for 450 respondents to +/-9.8% for 100 respondents. Subgroups of less than 100 were not included unless the variables were subsequently recoded into larger groups.

For the Jacksonville survey, 948 interviews were conducted for the original sample. The same screening questions were utilized as in the Southern survey. Additionally, 260 interviews were conducted with African Americans from Jacksonville by random selection and combined with the other African American completions to create an oversample. The overall sample has a margin of error of +/-3.2%. The African American oversample has a margin of error of +/-5.1%. The Jacksonville survey was weighted for gender and party registration with population parameters provided by the Supervisor of Elections Office in Duval County. Overall results of these surveys are available in Appendix B. Different questions yield different frequencies because not all respondents were asked every question and some respondents chose not to answer some questions.

Note that the totals of some columns in the tables do not add up to 100.0% due to rounding, which is standard practice.

Appendix B

Questionnaire

Q1 Are you registered to vote?

	South[a]	Jacksonville[b]
1. Yes	100.0%	100.0%
2. No—terminate	0.0%	0.0%

[a] $N = 803$
[b] $N = 948$

Q2 Did you vote in the 2000 presidential election?

	South[a]	Jacksonville[b]
1. Yes	100.0%	100.0%
2. No—terminate	0.0%	0.0%

[a] $N = 803$
[b] $N = 948$

Q3 What are your chances of voting in the election for president this year?

	South[a]	Jacksonville[b]
1. Almost certain to vote	93.1%	N/A
2. Will probably vote	6.9%	N/A
3. Will probably not vote—terminate	0.0%	N/A
4. Will definitely not vote—terminate	0.0%	N/A

[a] $N = 803$
[b] Not applicable. This question not asked in the Jacksonville survey.

Q4 Suppose the general election were held today, and the candidates were George W. Bush, a Republican, and John Kerry, a Democrat. For whom would you vote?

	South[a]	Jacksonville[b]
1. Kerry—skip to Q6	38.1%	N/A
2. Bush—skip to Q6	47.6%	N/A
3. Someone else	2.3%	N/A
98. Unsure	8.4%	N/A
99. Refused	3.5%	N/A

[a] N = 803

[b] Not applicable. This question not asked in the Jacksonville survey.

Q5 As of today, do you lean more toward Bush, the Republican, or Kerry, the Democrat?

	South[a]	Jacksonville[b]
1. Bush	24.3%	N/A
2. Kerry	26.1%	N/A
98. Do not know	34.8%	N/A
99. Refused	14.8%	N/A

[a] N = 115

[b] Not applicable. This question not asked in the Jacksonville survey.

Q6 Do you consider yourself to be a Southerner?

	South[a]	Jacksonville[b]
1. Yes	74.5%	69.6%
2. No	25.0%	29.3%
98. Do not know	0.2%	0.4%
99. Refused	0.2%	0.6%

[a] N = 803

[b] N = 948

Q7 In what region of the country did you live when you were 6 years old?

	South[a]	Jacksonville[b]
1. South	64.2%	59.3%
2. Northeast	16.0%	20.7%
3. Midwest	10.9%	11.7%
4. Central Plains	1.6%	0.6%
5. Mountain West	1.1%	0.3%
6. West Coast	2.9%	2.3%

7. Other	2.8%	4.7%
98. Do not know	0.5%	0.2%
99. Refused	0.0%	0.1%

[a] N = 803
[b] N = 948

Q8 How long have you lived in the South?

	South[a]	Jacksonville[b]
1. Less than a year	1.9%	2.0%
2. 1 to 5 years	3.6%	13.7%
3. 6 to 10 years	4.7%	10.6%
4. 11 to 20 years	9.1%	17.8%
5. More than 20 years	31.6%	32.1%
6. Native of the South—skip to Q10	48.8%	23.7%
99. Refused	0.3%	0.0%

[a] N = 803
[b] N = 948

Q9 Why did you move to the South?

	South[a]	Jacksonville[b]
1. Family	35.8%	36.6%
2. Weather	13.3%	5.9%
3. Economic opportunities	19.0%	32.2%
4. Other	29.8%	24.4%
98. Do not know	1.4%	0.8%
99. Refused	0.7%	0.0%

[a] N = 803
[b] N = 948

Q10 With which political party are you registered?

	South[a]	Jacksonville[b]
1. Democrat	41.7%	43.9%
2. Republican	36.3%	40.0%
3. Independent—skip to Q12	14.2%	10.7%
4. Other	5.1%	3.0%
98. Do not know	1.9%	0.6%
99. Refused	0.9%	1.7%

[a] N = 803
[b] N = 948

Q11 Which political party do you identify with?

	South[a]	Jacksonville[b]
1. Democrat	41.4%	33.6%
2. Republican	41.4%	47.0%
3. Independent—skip to Q14	4.9%	9.1%
4. Other	6.5%	6.1%
98. Do not know	4.4%	2.4%
99. Refused	1.4%	1.8%

[a] $N = 803$

[b] $N = 948$

Note: Identification compiled by combining independents from Q10 and Q11.

Q12 Do you consider yourself a strong Democrat/Republican or a not-very-strong Democrat/Republican?

	South[a]	Jacksonville[b]
1. Strong	66.3%	71.7%
2. Not very strong	30.9%	26.3%
99. Refused	2.8%	2.0%

[a] $N = 570$

[b] $N = 764$

Q13 As an independent, do you lean toward the Democrats, or more toward the Republicans? (Asked of independents only)

	South[a]	Jacksonville[b]
1. Democrats	23.1%	35.7%
2. Republicans	41.9%	28.6%
3. Neither—truly independent	33.8%	22.2%
98. Do not know	0.0%	6.5%
99. Refused	1.2%	7.0%

[a] $N = 148$

[b] $N = 185$

Q14 In the last 20 years, have you switched political parties?

	South[a]	Jacksonville[b]
1. Yes	18.8%	17.2%
2. No—skip to Q16	80.5%	82.4%
99. Refused—skip to Q16	0.7%	0.4%

[a] $N = 803$
[b] $N = 948$

Q15 What is the most important reason you switched political parties?

	South[a]	Jacksonville[b]
1. Did not agree with party's economic policies	18.3%	8.5%
2. Did not agree with party's stand on cultural issues	13.3%	16.5%
3. Did not agree with party on national security issues	2.9%	4.3%
4. Did not like party leadership	24.1%	32.9%
5. Other	36.4%	36.6%
98. Do not know	5.0%	1.2%

[a] $N = 164$
[b] $N = 151$

Q16 In terms of your religion, are you:

	South[a]	Jacksonville[b]
1. Protestant	61.7%	47.5%
2. Catholic	14.9%	16.4%
3. Jewish	2.4%	1.6%
4. Other	15.7%	22.5%
5. Not religious or atheist	4.3%	10.1%
99. Refused	1.0%	1.5%
98. Do not know	0.0%	0.3%

Note: Many other respondents included either nondenominational or church types that could not be identified.

Q17 When it comes to your religious faith, do you consider yourself a:

	South[a]	Jacksonville[b]
1. Charismatic	7.0%	N/A
2. Fundamentalist	7.5%	N/A
3. Evangelical	10.5%	N/A
4. Mainline Protestant	20.6%	N/A
5. Theologically liberal	12.8%	N/A
6. Other	29.2%	N/A
98. Do not know	11.9%	N/A
99. Refused	0.5%	N/A

[a] $N = 621$

[b] N = Not applicable. This question not asked in the Jacksonville survey.

Q18 About how often do you attend church or religious services?

	South[a]	Jacksonville[b]
1. More than once a week	21.1%	17.0%
2. Once a week	38.6%	32.7%
3. Once a month	19.7%	8.1%
4. Twice per month	N/A	9.7%
5. A few times a year	N/A	14.6%
6. Once per year	9.9%	4.3%
7. Do not attend church	9.5%	12.4%
98. Do not know	0.7%	0.0%
99. Refused	0.6%	1.1%

[a] $N = 621$

[b] $N = 948$

Q19 Most African Americans in the South support the Democratic Party, while many white Southerners support the Republican Party. Does this political difference harm race relations in the South?

	South[a]	Jacksonville[b]
1. Yes	21.5%	30.4%
2. No	61.1%	56.5%
98. Do not know	16.6%	11.2%
99. Refused	0.8%	1.9%

[a] $N = 803$

[b] $N = 948$

Q20 Do you believe that African Americans in the South (or Jacksonville) experience racial discrimination in their daily lives?

	South[a]	Jacksonville[b]
1. Yes	56.6%	56.6%
2. No	37.4%	33.8%
98. Do not know	5.5%	8.5%
99. Refused	0.5%	1.1%

[a] $N = 803$
[b] $N = 948$

Q21 How important are elected political officials in helping to improve race relations?

	South[a]	Jacksonville[b]
1. Very important	44.9%	54.3%
2. Somewhat important	30.9%	25.7%
3. Somewhat unimportant	11.5%	7.7%
4. Very unimportant	7.8%	7.2%
98. Do not know	4.5%	4.3%
99. Refused	0.3%	0.8%

[a] $N = 803$
[b] $N = 948$

Q22 With Republicans winning many elections across the South, do you believe under Republican leadership that race relations between whites and African Americans will:

	South[a]	Jacksonville[b]
1. Improve	26.1%	28.0%
2. Get worse	14.0%	13.0%
3. Remain the same	50.7%	50.2%
98. Do not know	8.6%	7.1%
99. Refused	0.6%	1.8%

[a] $N = 803$
[b] $N = 948$

Q23 Which of the following responses is closer to your view about affirmative action?

	South[a]	Jacksonville[b]
1. Affirmative action is needed in our society to assist African Americans and other minorities due to a pattern of historical discrimination	34.0%	37.9%
2. Affirmative action is not needed in our society because it represents an unconstitutional practice of racial preferences	52.4%	50.9%
98. Do not know	11.7%	8.9%
99. Refused	1.9%	2.3%

[a] $N = 803$
[b] $N = 948$

Q24 How important is it to you that elected officials have strong moral character? Is it . . .

	South[a]	Jacksonville[b]
1. Very important	78.5%	83.1%
2. Somewhat important	15.7%	11.5%
3. Somewhat unimportant	2.7%	2.0%
4. Very unimportant	2.1%	1.9%
98. Do not know	0.7%	1.2%
99. Refused	0.3%	0.3%

[a] $N = 803$
[b] $N = 948$

Q25 Which political party has more leaders who have strong moral character?

	South[a]	Jacksonville[b]
1. Democrats	20.4%*	19.2%
2. Republicans	35.9%	42.3%
3. Other	0.0%	1.0%
4. About the same	19.3%	12.1%
5. None	0.0%	10.5%
98. Do not know	23.4%	12.5%

99. Refused	0.9%	2.4%

[a] $N = 756$
[b] $N = 899$

Q26 How concerned are you that the moral values of the United States are declining?

	South[a]	Jacksonville[b]
1. Very concerned	68.7%	69.0%
2. Somewhat concerned	20.9%	18.1%
3. Somewhat unconcerned	4.7%	5.7%
4. Very unconcerned	3.5%	4.1%
98. Do not know	2.0%	2.4%
99. Refused	0.3%	0.4%

[a] $N = 803$
[b] $N = 948$

Q27 Which political party is more family-friendly?

	South[a]	Jacksonville[b]
1. Democrats	34.3%	34.1%
2. Republicans	36.2%	39.2%
3. Other	0.0%	3.9%
4. About the same/none	7.1%	8.4%
98. Do not know	21.5%	11.8%
99. Refused	0.9%	2.5%

[a] $N = 803$
[b] $N = 948$

Q28 Do you support or oppose allowing same-sex couples the right to get married?

	South[a]	Jacksonville[b]
1. Support	23.0%	22.9%
2. Oppose	68.9%	68.9%
98. Do not know	6.7%	6.7%
99. Refused	1.5%	1.5%

[a] $N = 803$
[b] $N = 948$

Q29 On the issue of abortion, are you more pro-life or more pro-choice?

	South[a]	Jacksonville[b]
1. Pro-life	49.5%	49.1%
2. Pro-choice	45.1%	44.4%
98. Do not know	4.4%	5.0%
99. Refused	0.9%	1.6%

[a] $N = 803$
[b] $N = 948$

Q30 Do you favor tougher gun-control laws in this country?

	South[a]	Jacksonville[b]
1. Yes	51.6%	54.4%
2. No	42.8%	41.2%
98. Do not know	5.5%	3.7%
99. Refused	0.1%	0.6%

[a] $N = 803$
[b] $N = 948$

Q31 Do you support or oppose President Bush's decision to go to war with Iraq in March of 2003?

	South[a]	Jacksonville[b]
1. Strongly support	41.1%	44.1%
2. Somewhat support	16.0%	13.1%
3. Somewhat oppose	10.6%	8.8%
4. Strongly oppose	28.7%	31.1%
98. Do not know	3.2%	2.2%
99. Refused	0.4%	0.7%

[a] $N = 803$
[b] $N = 948$

Q32 How important are your religious values in determining your political beliefs? Are they . . .

	South[a]	Jacksonville[b]
1. Very important	45.8%	46.6%
2. Somewhat important	28.7%	26.2%
3. Somewhat unimportant	10.1%	11.6%
4. Very unimportant	14.3%	15.1%

98. Do not know	0.6%	0.5%
99. Refused	0.5%	0.1%

[a] $N = 768$
[b] $N = 856$

Q33 How important is it to you that the president of the United States be a religious person? Is it . . .

	South[a]	Jacksonville[b]
1. Very important	50.4%	48.2%
2. Somewhat important	25.3%	24.6%
3. Somewhat unimportant	8.9%	11.0%
4. Very unimportant	10.7%	14.7%
98. Do not know	2.1%	1.3%
99. Refused	0.0%	0.3%

[a] $N = 803$
[b] $N = 948$

Q34 Do you think the Democratic/Republican Party is sinful?

	South[a]	Jacksonville[b]
1. Yes	26.5%	25.2%
2. No	59.2%	59.0%
98. Do not know	12.0%	10.6%
99. Refused	2.3%	5.2%

[a] $N = 667$
[b] $N = 763$

Q35 Agree or disagree? Religious leaders should stay out of politics and public affairs.

	South[a]	Jacksonville[b]
1. Strongly agree	32.6%	30.9%
2. Somewhat agree	17.2%	15.7%
3. Somewhat disagree	21.0%	20.5%
4. Strongly disagree	25.0%	29.5%
98. Do not know	3.6%	2.6%
99. Refused	0.7%	0.4%

[a] $N = 803$
[b] $N = 948$

Q36 Agree or disagree? Generally, Southerners have stronger moral values than other people in the country.

	South[a]	Jacksonville[b]
1. Strongly agree	17.9%	N/A
2. Somewhat agree	14.9%	N/A
3. Somewhat disagree	24.8%	N/A
4. Strongly disagree	31.3%	N/A
98. Do not know	10.2%	N/A
99. Refused	0.9%	N/A

[a] $N = 803$

[b] Not applicable. This question not asked in the Jacksonville survey.

Q37 In which region of the country do people have the weakest moral values?

	South[a]	Jacksonville[b]
1. South	3.7%	N/A
2. Northeast	10.4%	N/A
3. Midwest	1.1%	N/A
4. Central Plains	0.5%	N/A
5. Mountain West	0.6%	N/A
6. West Coast	43.2%	N/A
98. Do not know	37.1%	N/A
99. Refused	3.4%	N/A

[a] $N = 803$

[b] Not applicable. This question not asked in the Jacksonville survey.

Q38 Which of the following statements is closer to your view of government?

	South[a]	Jacksonville[b]
1. Government is necessary to provide the rules and regulations that are needed to provide order in American society.	69.8%	N/A
2. Government makes rules and regulations that take away from individual freedom and end up harming American society.	19.1%	N/A
98. Do not know	10.0%	N/A
99. Refused	1.1%	N/A

[a] $N = 803$

[b] Not applicable. This question not asked in the Jacksonville survey.

Q39 Would you rather have the federal government or the state government handle important political issues that matter to you?

	South[a]	Jacksonville[b]
1. Federal government	35.3%	30.1%
2. State government	46.3%	51.9%
3. Local government (Not read. Offered only in Jacksonville survey.)	N/A	3.9%
98. Do not know	16.5%	12.0%
99. Refused	1.8%	2.1%

[a] $N = 803$
[b] $N = 948$

Q40 Agree or disagree? More tax cuts are needed to help the economy.

	South[a]	Jacksonville[b]
1. Strongly agree	25.7%	31.0%
2. Somewhat agree	16.4%	18.4%
3. Somewhat disagree	22.6%	18.8%
4. Strongly disagree	28.1%	25.1%
98. Do not know	6.6%	5.8%
99. Refused	0.7%	0.8%

[a] $N = 803$
[b] $N = 948$

Q41 Which political party do you trust more on national security and defense issues?

	South[a]	Jacksonville[b]
1. Republicans	47.9%	54.8%
2. Democrats	29.8%	26.0%
3. Neither	8.4%	9.1%
4. Both equally	6.0%	4.2%
98. Do not know	6.7%	4.3%
99. Refused	1.2%	1.6%

[a] $N = 803$
[b] $N = 948$

Q42 Which political party do you trust more on economic issues?

	South[a]	Jacksonville[b]
1. Republicans	40.1%	49.5%
2. Democrats	42.8%	37.0%
3. Neither	7.8%	6.8%
4. Both equally	3.2%	2.6%
98. Do not know	5.1%	2.7%
99. Refused	1.0%	1.4%

[a] $N = 803$
[b] $N = 948$

Q43 Which political party do you trust more on moral and cultural issues?

	South[a]	Jacksonville[b]
1. Republicans	40.6%	46.5%
2. Democrats	30.3%	32.1%
3. Neither	14.6%	10.2%
4. Both equally	5.1%	6.3%
98. Do not know	7.7%	3.4%
99. Refused	1.7%	1.5%

[a] $N = 803$
[b] $N = 948$

Q44 Which is more important for the government to do: protecting the environment or helping economic growth?

	South[a]	Jacksonville[b]
1. Protecting the environment	25.7%	28.0%
2. Helping economic growth	45.4%	39.5%
3. Neither	1.2%	0.7%
4. Both equally	25.1%	28.6%
98. Do not know	1.6%	2.6%
99. Refused	1.0%	0.6%

[a] $N = 803$
[b] $N = 948$

Q45 Are you satisfied or dissatisfied with the environmental protection within 1 mile of your home?

	South[a]	Jacksonville[b]
1. Very satisfied	46.5%	42.7%
2. Somewhat satisfied	28.5%	30.1%
3. Somewhat dissatisfied	10.0%	9.1%
4. Very dissatisfied	13.0%	16.0%
98. Do not know	1.9%	1.6%
99. Refused	0.1%	0.5%

[a] $N = 803$
[b] $N = 948$

Q46 Which political party better represents the interests of working people?

	South[a]	Jacksonville[b]
1. Democrats	49.8%	46.6%
2. Republicans	32.5%	35.4%
3. Neither	4.4%	6.9%
4. Both equally	4.5%	4.2%
98. Do not know	7.9%	5.3%
99. Refused	0.9%	1.6%

[a] $N = 803$
[b] $N = 948$

Q47 Which political party helps the lower class more?

	South[a]	Jacksonville[b]
1. Democrats	61.1%	58.8%
2. Republicans	20.8%	25.0%
3. Neither	4.7%	5.7%
4. Both equally	3.9%	3.4%
98. Do not know	8.2%	6.0%
99. Refused	1.3%	1.2%

[a] $N = 803$
[b] $N = 948$

Q48 Which political party helps the middle class more?

	South[a]	Jacksonville[b]
1. Democrats	40.6%	37.2%
2. Republicans	36.4%	45.7%
3. Neither	7.4%	6.8%
4. Both equally	5.3%	4.1%
98. Do not know	9.2%	5.0%
99. Refused	1.1%	1.2%

[a] $N = 803$
[b] $N = 948$

Q49 Which political party helps the upper class more?

	South[a]	Jacksonville[b]
1. Democrats	6.2%	10.5%
2. Republicans	78.0%	78.3%
3. Neither	3.0%	2.5%
4. Both equally	3.6%	3.1%
98. Do not know	7.5%	4.3%
99. Refused	1.7%	1.3%

[a] $N = 803$
[b] $N = 948$

Q50 In terms of your political ideology, are you liberal, moderate, or conservative?

	South[a]	Jacksonville[b]
1. Liberal	16.5%	15.9%
2. Moderate	36.3%	39.6%
3. Conservative	43.1%	42.0%
98. Do not know	3.5%	2.0%
99. Refused	0.6%	0.5%

[a] $N = 803$
[b] $N = 948$

Q51 On a scale of 1 to 100, with 1 representing "cold" feelings and 100 being "very warm" feelings, how do you feel about George W. Bush?

Mean = 56.27

Q52 Using the same scale of 1 to 100, how do you feel about Bill Clinton?

Mean = 43.43

Q53 Using the same scale, how do you feel about Ronald Reagan?

Mean = 64.33

Q54 On the same scale of 1 to 100, how do you feel about Franklin Delano Roosevelt?

Mean = 70.34

Q55 These last few questions are so we can compare your answers to others in the survey. What is your race or ethnic background? Is it:

	South[a]	Jacksonville[b]
1. White	78.8%	69.7%
2. Black or African American	14.1%	21.9%
3. Asian	0.4%	1.1%
4. Other	5.6%	5.2%
99. Refused	1.1%	2.1%

[a] $N = 803$
[b] $N = 948$

Q56 Are you of Hispanic or Latino origin?

	South[a]	Jacksonville[b]
1. Yes	5.0%	3.8%
2. No	94.7%	94.9%
99. Refused	0.4%	1.3%

[a] $N = 803$
[b] $N = 948$

Q57 What is the highest grade in school or year of college you have completed?

	South[a]	Jacksonville[b]
1. Grade school	3.3%	2.7%
2. High school graduate	19.4%	20.1%
3. Some college	30.0%	31.0%
4. College graduate	28.9%	29.9%
5. Postgraduate degree	18.3%	15.9%
99. Refused	0.0%	0.3%

[a] $N = 803$
[b] $N = 948$

Q58 How would you describe the area in which you live? Would you say . . .

	South[a]	Jacksonville[b]
1. Urban	22.5%	30.4%
2. Suburban	30.9%	57.3%
3. Rural	19.6%	6.8%
4. Small town	26.0%	4.4%
99. Refused	0.9%	1.1%

[a] N = 803
[b] N = 948

Q59 What is your current age?

	South[a]	Jacksonville[b]
1. 18 to 30	9.9%	N/A
2. 31 to 40	18.3%	N/A
3. 41 to 50	26.0%	N/A
4. 51 to 60	21.9%	N/A
5. 61 or older	23.3%	N/A
99. Refused	0.7%	N/A

[a] N = 674
[b] Not applicable. This question not asked in the Jacksonville survey.

Q60 What was your total household income in 2003? Was it:

	South[a]	Jacksonville[b]
1. Less than $20,000	12.2%	8.4%
2. $20,000 to $50,000	28.5%	29.2%
3. $50,000 to $100,000	32.8%	35.5%
4. More than $100,000	16.6%	17.3%
99. Refused	9.9%	9.5%

[a] N = 803
[b] N = 948

Q61 Respondent gender (weighted)

	South[a]	Jacksonville[b]
1. Male	48.0%	48.1%
2. Female	52.0%	51.9%

[a] N = 803
[b] N = 948

Notes

Chapter 1. Introduction

1. Exit polls of the South are available at CNN.com and MSNBC.com.

2. The influx of Hispanic immigrants is another reason the percentage of native Southerners is declining.

Chapter 2. Case Study: Jacksonville, Florida

1. As of this writing, the current state attorney is a Democrat, but his circuit encompasses more than one county.

2. For a comprehensive look at consolidation, consult *Jacksonville: The Consolidation Story from Civil Rights to the Jaguars,* by historian Jim Crooks.

3. See Appendixes A and B for question wording and study methodology.

Chapter 3. The Politics of Resegregation

1. In 2005, then-governor Jeb Bush appointed a special prosecutor to reopen this case.

2. Professor Stephen Baker of Jacksonville University did the primary research on these numbers. He has performed extensive research on the 2000 Presidential race in Jacksonville.

Chapter 4. Southern Religion Meets Modern Politics

1. Wilcox includes an excellent glossary on religious terms in his book *Onward Christian Soldiers.*

Works Cited

Abcarian, R. 2005. Faithful celebrate Bush right. *Los Angeles Times*, January 21.

Aistrup, Joseph A. 1996. *The Southern strategy revisited: Republican top-down advancement in the South.* Lexington: University of Kentucky Press.

Alter, Jonathan. 2006. Bush still blind to the poverty. Associated Press, August 29.

Applebome, Peter. 1996. *Dixie rising: How the South is shaping American values, politics, and culture.* New York: Random House.

Associated Press. 2005. Half of Alabama public school students now in poverty. May 11.

Austin, Kevin S. 2005. Church torn by political ultimatum. *Atlanta Journal-Constitution*, May 8, A1.

Bai, Matt. 2005. Democratic moral values. *New York Times*, April 24.

Bartley, Abel. 2000. *Keeping the faith: Race, politics, and social development in Jacksonville, Florida, 1940–1970.* Westport, Conn.: Greenwood Press.

Basch, Mark. 2003. Fidelity confirms its sights on Duval. *Florida Times-Union*, April 23, sec. B.

Bass, Jack and Walter DeVries. 1975. *The transformation of Southern politics: Social change and political consequence since 1945.* New York: Basic Books.

Bauerlein, David. 1998. Run over no more pine forest to join intensive care project. *Florida Times-Union*, April 29.

Bibby, John F. and Brian F. Schaffner. 2000. *Politics, parties, and elections in America.* Belmont, Cal.: Wadsworth.

Black, Earl and Merle Black. 1987. *Politics and society in the South.* Cambridge, Mass.: Harvard University Press.

———. 1992. *The vital South.* Cambridge, Mass.: Harvard University Press.

———. 2000. *The rise of Southern Republicans.* Cambridge, Mass.: Harvard University Press.

Bositis, David. 2001. *Black elected officials.* Washington, D.C.: Joint Center for Political and Economic Studies.

Brattain, Michelle. 2002. *The politics of whiteness.* Princeton, N.J.: Princeton University Press.

Brown, Corrine. 2004. Speech to the mock political convention. Prime Osborne Center, Jacksonville, Fla. February 20.

Brumley, Jeff. 2004a. Edwards, ex-Christian Coalition leader, brings political messages to churches. *Florida Times-Union*, November 1.

———. 2004b. Moral values; swayed voters to choose Bush. *Florida Times-Union*, November 4.

———. 2004c. Catholics set to aid Baptists to fight gay vows. *Florida Times-Union*, December 12.

————. 2005. Rove tells Vines that Miers is a good pick. *Florida Times-Union,* October 15, sec. A.

————. 2006. Atheists file lawsuit over Day of Faith. *Florida Times-Union,* September 2.

Bullock, Charles S., III, and Mark J. Rozell. 2003. Southern politics in the twenty-first century. In *The new politics of the Old South: An introduction to Southern politics,* 3rd ed. Edited by Bullock and Rozell. Lanham, Md.: Rowman and Littlefield.

Busmiller, Elizabeth and Anne Kornblut. 2005. Black leaders say storm forced Bush to confront issues of race and poverty. *New York Times,* September 18.

Button, James. 1989. *Blacks and social change: The impact of the Civil Rights Act in six Southern communities.* Princeton, N.J.: Princeton University Press.

Carmines, Edward G. and James A. Stimson. 1989. *Issue evolution: Race and the transformation of American politics.* Princeton, N.J.: Princeton University Press.

Carter, Dan. 2000. *The politics of rage: George Wallace, the origins of the new conservatism, and the transformation of American politics.* Baton Rouge: Louisiana State University Press.

Clubock, Alfred, John Degrove, and Charles Farris. 1964. The manipulated Negro vote: Some preconditions and consequences. *Journal of Politics* 26: 112–29.

Conrad, Jarik. 2005. *Blueprint for prosperity: Public input draft.* <www.myjaxchamber. com/Blueprint/DraftPlan.pdf/> (accessed January 3, 2006).

Corrigan, Matthew T. 2000. Top-down Republicanism in the South: A view from the local level. *State and Local Government Review* 32, 1 (Winter 2000): 61–69.

Council of Social Agencies, Jacksonville, Florida. 1946. Jacksonville looks at its Negro community: A survey of conditions affecting the Negro population in Jacksonville and Duval County, Florida. Facsimile PDF available online at AmericanSouth.org. <www.americansouth.org/viewrecord.php?id=25492>.

Crooks, James. 2004. *Jacksonville: The consolidation story from civil rights to the Jaguars.* Gainesville, Fla.: University Press of Florida.

Debose, Brian. 2004. Martinez believes pollsters in victory over McCollum. *Washington Post,* September 2, sec. A.

DeCamp, David. 2000. Heat is on election officials. *Florida Times-Union,* November 14, sec. A.

————. 2003a. Racial graffiti targets Glover campaign office. *Florida Times-Union,* May 4.

————. 2003b. Campaign's race factor heats up. *Florida Times-Union,* May 9.

————. 2004. Won't add early vote locations, Duval says. *Florida Times-Union,* October 12.

Dionne, E. J., Jr. and Kayla M. Drogosz. 2002. How would God vote? In *One electorate under God?: A dialogue on religion and American politics,* Edited by E. J. Dionne, Jean Bethke Elshtain, and Kayla Drogosz. Washington, D.C.: Brookings Institution Press.

Dodson, David, Alison Greene, Ferrel Guillory, Joan Lipsitz, and Sarah Rueben. 2004. *The state of the South: A report by MDC at Chapel Hill.* Chapel Hill, N.C.: MDC. <www.mdcinc.org/docs/sos_04.pdf/> (accessed December 10, 2005).

Ferguson, Niall. 2003. Why America outpaces Europe (clue: the God factor). *New York Times*, June 8.

Firestone, David. 2000. Bush is the brand of Republican South Carolina favors. *New York Times*, February 2.

Florida Times-Union. 1964. Large area is terrorized by Negroes. March 24, sec. A.

———. 1964. Arizonan hits Rights Act: Johnson raps extremism. November 3, sec. A.

———. 1964. Goldwater has the edge in North Florida. November 4, sec. A.

———. 1995. Racial bias enters mayor's race. May 6, sec. B.

Foner, Eric. 1988. *Reconstruction: America's unfinished revolution, 1863–1877*. New York: Harper and Row.

Fournier, Ron. 2004. For Kerry, a big night in the South, his last of the year. Associated Press Worldstream, March 9.

Frank, Thomas. 2004. *What's the matter with Kansas?* New York: Metropolitan Books.

Frey, William H. 1998. Black migration to the South reaches record highs in 1990s. *Population Today* 26 (2): reprint no. 561.

Fridell, Zach. 2005. Glory not gridiron at Jesus march. *Florida Times-Union,* January 30, sec. B.

Grammich, Clifford. 2005. *Swift growth and change: The demography of Southern Catholicism*. Washington, D.C.: Glenmary Research Center. <www.frinstitute.org/southern.htm/> (accessed January 15, 2006).

Greely, Andrew. 2002. Puritans and American politics. In *One electorate under God?: A dialogue on religion and American politics*. Edited by E. J. Dionne, Jean Bethke Elshtain, and Kayla Drogosz. Washington, D.C.: Brookings Institution Press.

Green, John C., Lyman A. Kellstedt, Corwin E. Smidt, and James L. Guth. 2003. *The soul of the South: Religion and Southern politics at the millennium*. Lanham, Md.: Rowman and Littlefield.

Green, John C., and James L Guth. 1991. The Bible and the ballot box: The shape of things to come. In *The Bible and the ballot box: Religion and politics in the 1988 election*. Edited by J. L Guth and J. C Green. Boulder, Colo.: Westview.

Greenberg, Stanley B. 2005. 1991: How we found—and lost—a majority. *American Prospect*, June.

Greenblatt, Alan. 2003. The two-sided South. *Governing Magazine*, July. <governing.com/textbook/south.htm/> (accessed June 20, 2005).

Hallifax, Jackie. 2003. High court says NAACP can challenge One Florida policies. Associated Press, November 13.

Halpern, Rick. 1997. Louisiana's sugar workers. In *Southern labor in transit*. Edited by Robert Zieger. 86–112. Knoxville, Tenn.: University of Tennessee Press.

Harvard, William C., ed. 1972. *The changing politics of the South*. Baton Rouge: Louisiana State University Press.

Heard, Alexander. 1952. *A two-party South?* Chapel Hill: University of North Carolina Press.

Hill, Patrice. 2005. Income gap grows in U.S. *Washington Times*, July 31.

Hill, Samuel. 1966. *Religion and the solid South*. Nashville: Abingdon Press.

Jacksonville Community Council. 2005. Quality of life progress report: A guide to building a better community. Jacksonville, Fla.: Jacksonville Community Council, Inc. <www.jcci.org/> (accessed December 1, 2005).

———. 2005. Race relations progress report. Jacksonville, Fla.: Jacksonville Community Council, Inc. <www.jcci.org/> (accessed December 15, 2005).

Johnson, Glen. 2004. Kerry camp on the defensive after celebrities bash Bush. Associated Press, July 10.

Keech, William. 1968. *The impact of Negro voting: The role of the vote in the quest for equality.* Chicago: Rand McNally.

Kelly, Joyce, and Michael Conlon. 2005. Megachurches draw big crowds. Reuters, November 22.

Key, V. O. 1949. *Southern politics in state and nation.* New York: Knopf.

King, Martin Luther, Jr. 1963. *Letter from a Birmingham jail.* Atlanta: The Estate of Martin Luther King Jr.

Kingdon, John. 1984. *Agendas, alternatives and public policies.* Boston: Little, Brown.

Ledbetter, James. 2004. *Dismantling persistent poverty in the Southern United States.* Washington, D.C.: Carl Vinson Institute of Government.

Leege, David, Kenneth Wald, Brian Krueger, and Paul Mueller. 2002. *The politics of cultural differences: Social change and voter mobilization in the post–New Deal period.* Princeton, N.J.: Princeton University Press.

Lester, Will. 2005. Military kin likelier to back war. Associated Press, August 26.

Lewis, Sinclair. 1929. *Cheap and contented labor: The picture of a Southern mill town in 1929.* New York: United Textile Workers of America and Women's Trade Union League.

Lublin, David. 1997. *The paradox of representation: Racial gerrymandering and minority interests in Congress.* Princeton, N.J.: Princeton University Press.

Maisel, Sandy L. 1999. *Parties and elections in America: The electoral process.* Lanham, Md.: Rowman and Littlefield.

Martin, Richard. 1972. *The city makers.* Jacksonville, Fla.: Convention Press.

Meyerson, Harold. 2005. ISO: working class Democrats. *Washington Post*, February 23, sec. A.

Morill, Richard. 2000. Geographic variation in change in income inequality among U.S. states, 1790–1990. *Annals of Regional Science* 34: 109–30.

Moynihan, Daniel P. 1996. *Miles to go: A personal history of social policy.* Boston, Mass.: Harvard University Press.

Murphy, Bridget. 2006. Peyton says no to a call for firings. *Florida Times-Union*, August 16.

———. 2006. Firehouse inquiry finds no culprits. *Florida Times-Union*, November 22.

Ortiz, Paul. 2005. *Emancipation betrayed: The hidden history of black organizing and white violence in Florida Reconstruction to the bloody election of 1920.* Los Angeles: University of California Press.

Pew Forum on Religion and Public Life. 2005. A faith-based partisan divide. In *Trends 2005*. Washington, D.C.: Pew Research Center. <pewforum.org/> (accessed February 25, 2005).

Pew Hispanic Center. 2005. The new Latino South: The context and consequences of rapid population growth. July 26. Washington, D.C.: Pew Research Center. <pewhispanic.org/reports/report.php?ReportID=5> (accessed February 22, 2006).

Pinkham, Paul. 2005. Parents ask judge to let Schiavo divorce husband. *Florida Times-Union*, March 1.

Pinzur, Matthew. 2002. Political leaders cautiously supportive. *Florida Times-Union*, June 12.

Raines, Howell. 1980. Reagan backs Evangelicals in their political activities. *New York Times*, August 23.

Reeves, Jay. 2003. Riley tax plan fared best in mostly black counties. Associated Press, September 10.

Reichley, A. James. 2002. *Faith in politics*. Washington, D.C.: Brookings Institution Press.

Rushing, Taylor. 2006. Black candidates face rarity. *Florida Times-Union*, July 20.

Sale, Kirpatrick. 1975. *Power shift: The rise of the Southern rim and its challenge to the Eastern establishment*. New York: Random House.

Schaller, Thomas. 2006. *Whistling past Dixie: How Democrats can win without the South*. New York: Simon and Schuster.

Scher, Richard. 1997. *Politics in the New South: Republicanism, race and leadership in the twentieth century*. New York: Paragon House.

Schoettler, Jim. 2006. Murder rate up, but outcry is missing. *Florida Times-Union*, April 2.

Schonger, Kathleen. 2006. Irish immigrants. In *Immigration in U.S. history*. Edited by Carl L. Bankston III, and Danielle Hidalgo. Salem, Mass.: Salem Press.

Shafer, Byron E. and Richard Johnson. 2006. *The end of Southern exceptionalism: Class, race and partisan change in the postwar South*. Cambridge, Mass.: Harvard University Press.

Shaffrey, Mary. 2005. Party rethinks take on abortion. *Winston-Salem Journal*, March 6.

Simon, Bryant. 1997. Rethinking why there are so many unions in the South. *Georgia Historical Quarterly* 81 (2): 465.

Straub, Noelle. 2004. Kerry takes up values theme in Ohio stumping. *Boston Herald*, August 2.

Thomas, Evan. 2006. A secret life: Mark Foley's explicit e-mails could bring down the GOP. His story, and the fallout. *Newsweek*, October 16.

United Press International. 2004. "South is mine," Bush says. July 7.

U.S. Government Accounting Office. 1990. *Case study evaluations*. Washington, D.C.: U.S. Government Printing Office.

Wald, Kenneth, Dennis Owen, and Samuel Hill. 1988. Churches as political communities. *American Political Science Review* 82 (2): 531–48.

Weathersbee, Tonyaa. 2006. A rebirth of black leadership is needed to stem tide of violence. *Florida Times-Union*, August 22.

Wilcox, Clyde. 1994. *Onward Christian soldiers.* London: Westview Press.

Yglesias, Matthew. 2006. Just what is the working class? *The American Prospect*, February: 40.

Zoll, Rachel. 2004. Republican request for church directories angers some religious leaders. Associated Press, July 23.

Index

Abortion: Jimmy Carter and, 62; John Kerry and, 10; as political issue, 8, 23, 84; and race, 72, 73; and religion, 8, 10, 62, 68, 69, 72, 73, 76, 84, 87; and *Roe v. Wade*, 62, 69, 73; as survey issue, 122

Affirmative action. *See* Discrimination: and affirmative action

African Americans: as business owners, 28; and civil rights movement, 29, 34, 45, 107; and Civil War and Reconstruction, 19, 27; and class, 11, 30, 31, 95, 97, 98, 99, 100, 101; and crime, 29, 30, 61; and discrimination and affirmative action, 6–7, 23, 32, 44, 45, 48, 52, 54, 55, 119; and economic opportunity, 30; and education, 7, 27, 29, 30, 31; as elected officials, 5, 25, 26, 27, 29, 39, 42, 47, 52, 53–54, 55, 107, 108; and elections, 6, 25–26, 32, 34, 48–51, 52; and franchise, 27, 28; and Great Society programs, 45, 46; and Hispanics, 56; and income, 93, 97, 103; as independent voters, 42; in Jacksonville/Duval County, 4, 21, 23, 34, 52, 100, 103, 112; and migration, 23–24, 28, 89; and New Deal, 13, 32, 34, 89; Northern, 91; occupations of, 30, 31, 77; and political activity, 4–5, 8, 26, 27, 28–29, 34, 41, 43, 55, 77, 86, 107; and poverty, 11, 14, 88, 109; and race relations, 32, 47–48, 53–54; and slavery, 27, 65; and social and political issues, 37, 46, 48, 54–55, 72, 73, 74, 78, 79, 82, 99; and standard of living, 30, 31, 108; surveys of, 4, 112, 129; and unions, 90, 98; and World Wars, 28. *See also* Democratic Party: African Americans and; Religion and morality: African Americans and; Republican Party: African Americans and

African Methodist, 78

Afro-American Insurance Company, 28

Alabama: African American elected officials in, 5; and Florida, 33; gambling in, 86; governors of, 109; map of, 18; political leaders from, 43; poor and poverty in, 15, 83–84, 88, 109; and presidential elections, 2; race in, 27; religion and morality in, 83–84; Republican Party in, 109; and segregation, 5; surveys in, 76, 111; taxes in, 83–84

American Catholic Church. *See* Catholics

Anderson, John, 36

Arkansas, 2, 15, 111

Atlanta, Ga., 90

Baker, Stephen, 131n1 (chap. 3)

Baptists: conservatives as, 63; and Democratic Party, 69; and government, 82; in Jacksonville/Duval County, 65, 67, 68, 69; and political activity, 63; and presidential elections, 35, 58; and Republican Party, 69; roles of, 81–82; and segregation, 65, 66; whites as, 77–78

Bartley, Abel, 29, 34

Bass, Jack, 2

Bennett, Charles, 38

Bethel Baptist Church (Jacksonville, Fla.), 65

Biomedical industries, 90–91

Birmingham, Ala., 61

Black, Earl, 2, 13, 18, 43, 45, 58, 91

Black, Merle, 2, 13, 18, 43, 45, 58, 91

Blueprint for Prosperity, 103

Brown, Corrine, 25, 39

Bullock, Charles S., III, 2–3, 19

Burns, Haydon, 21, 29

Bush, George W.: and 2000 presidential election, 1, 6, 8, 20, 48, 51, 63, 66, 71; and 2004 presidential election, 1, 6, 8, 9–10, 58, 59, 71, 114; approval ratings for, 23, 24, 37, 128; and Hurricane Katrina, 104–5; and Medicare, 104; and religion, 63; and war on terror, 80

Bush, Jeb, 7, 20, 37, 56–57, 131n1 (chap. 3)

Carlberg, Dick, 26

Carl Vinson Institute, 88

Carmines, Edward, 3–4

Matthew Corrigan is an associate professor of Political Science and Public Administration at the University of North Florida. He directs the Public Opinion Research Laboratory at the university. He has written and commented extensively on elections and public issues in Florida and the South. He is currently president of the Florida Political Science Association, a group of 60 political scientists from across the state. He has been cited as an expert on Florida politics in many newspapers and press outlets, including the *New York Times*, the Associated Press, CNN, the *Tampa Tribune*, and the *Tallahassee Democrat*. Corrigan has conducted numerous surveys on important issues on the state and local levels in Florida and in the South. He also served as an expert witness in reviewing election procedures in Duval County. He lives in Jacksonville, Florida, with his wife, Mary, and son, John.